# Tell Me Your Name

## Images of God in the Bible

# Tell Me Your Name

## Images of God in the Bible

Arthur E. Zannoni

LTP

LITURGY
TRAINING
PUBLICATIONS

TELL ME YOUR NAME: IMAGES OF GOD IN THE BIBLE © 2000 Archdiocese of Chicago: Liturgy Training Publications, 1800 North Hermitage Avenue, Chicago, Illinois 60622-1101; Telephone.: 1-800-933-1800; orders@ltp.org; fax: 1-800-933-7094. All rights reserved. Visit our website at www.ltp.org.

All scriptural quotations are from the *New Revised Standard Version Bible, Catholic Edition,* © 1993 and 1989, by the Division of Christian Education of the National Council of Churches of Christ in the United States of America. Published by Catholic Bible Press, a division of Thomas Nelson, Inc., Nashville, Tennessee, U.S.A., 37214. Used with permission. All rights reserved.

Victoria M. Tufano edited this book. The production editor was Mariano Torrespico Ortíz. The designer was Larry Cope, and the production artist was Kari Nicholls. Printed by WEBCOM, Limited, Ontario, Canada. The art is by Julie Lonneman.

Cataloging-in-Publications Data. Printed in Canada. 00-100383

00  01  02  03  04  05  06    5  4  3  2  1

# Table of Contents

# ACKNOWLEDGMENTS

No publication is ever the result of just one individual's work. The idea for this book resulted from an adult education program I conducted at St. Olaf Catholic Church in downtown Minneapolis, Minnesota, and I would like to express my appreciation to Father John Forliti, the pastor, and to Mark Croteau, the Director of Programs, at the parish.

I want to thank Victoria Tufano of Liturgy Training Publications for her supportive encouragement and careful editing of the original manuscript; Leslie Carney for her attentive ear, enterprising spirit and expert typing of the manuscript; my fellow writers and dear friends, Bill Huebsch and David Haas for their constant support; and Richard M. Rose for his friendship and confidence in me.

Finally, I must express heartfelt appreciation to Kathleen Flannery Zannoni, my wife and fellow pilgrim on life's journey, for her love, care, affirmation and confidence in me throughout the tedious process called writing. Without her constant support, this book would never have been completed.

# THIS BOOK IS DEDICATED TO:

Kathleen Flannery Zannoni

Laura Charlene Zannoni Long

Luke Andrew Zannoni

Benjamino Maggie Zannoni

Alessandro Flannery Zannoni

Remember them in life, and health, and strength,

Lord who delights in life,

and inscribe them in the Book of Life

for all eternity.

# Introduction

All of us who take religion and faith as a serious part of our lives constantly wrestle with the meaning of God.

Searching for God has been compared to hunting a fox: elusive and impossible to catch but who can be glimpsed, from time to time, in a thicket or dense forest. Such sightings are quite exciting and awesome for the hunter of the holy mystery of God. While often elusive and mysterious, God is, nevertheless, the driving force in our lives. Searching for God, the divine fox, is part of our very existence.

Searching for God leads us to many resources. Some of us discover God in nature or in poetry or in literature while others seek God's image in fellow human beings; still others turn to the holy Bible. Even it, however, does not provide clear-cut answers about who God is; rather, it presents a plurality of images for God. Ultimately, God is beyond human comprehension and is not reducible to any one image, so the Bible offers many lenses with which to see God because no one lens provides a definitive image, just angles of vision.

Just as the solar system centers on the sun, so the Bible centers on God. God is not only the Bible's author but also its chief character. The Bible never proves God's existence but simply grants it. It does not contain systematic doctrines but rather testimonies to God as a living, personal being reaching out for responses throughout our history. As the Jewish theologian Abraham Joshua Heschel put it, the Bible does not present the "unmoved mover" of Aristotle but the "most moved mover"(*Between God and Man,* New York: Harpers, 1959, 24). It contains a vast range of responses to God, from praise of the creator through joy in the presence of God, to agonizing cries to a seemingly absent God. The Bible itself sanctions diverse responses to the mystery of God's existence, presence and love.

The biblical writers are God-intoxicated, God-possessed and God-articulate. They insist that God is more than a blur of longing and a monosyllabic noun. The God of whom they write is quite capable of intelligent discourse. Yet God is not so readily knowable as to become predictable, or so thoroughly known that there is no more for us to learn. The God of the Bible is known and unknown, rational and irrational, orderly and disorderly, hierarchical and anarchical.

There are tendencies within us and forces outside ourselves that relentlessly try to reduce God to a checklist of explanations or a handbook of moral precepts, an economic arrangement or even a political expediency. If God is reduced to what can be measured and weighed, gathered and controlled, felt or used, then, to the extent that we accept such reductionism, we become bored and depressed or mean. We grow stunted, like acorns in a terrarium. Just as oaks need soil and rain and sun and wind, human life requires God. The Bible speaks in such a way that God is not reduced or packaged but rather known and contemplated and adored, with the consequence that our lives are exalted by whom we worship and not cramped into what we can explain.

The difficulties surrounding thought about God are formidable. The Christian community needs the biblical writers who keep us thinking about God instead of just guessing randomly. We require a God whom we can worship with our minds and hearts and strength. The taste for eternity can never be bred out of us by a secularizing genetics. Our existence is derived from and destined for God.

When God is the subject, some people become cautious, defining every term and qualifying every statement. They say no more than can be verified with logic. They do not want to be found guilty of speaking nonsense. Others, knowing how easily we drift into pious fantasies when God is the subject, become excessively practical. They turn every godly truth into a moral precept. The poets, prophets and sages of the Bible are extravagant and bold in abandoning both the caution of the religious philosopher and the earnestness of the ethical moralist. They use words to intensify our relationship with God. They are not trying to make us think more accurately or to train us in better behavior; instead, they try to get us to believe recklessly about God. The biblical authors work to jar us from our lethargy, to provoke us to alertness, to open our eyes to the fiery bush, to open our ears to the marvelous parables of Jesus, to banish boredom from the gospel, and to lift our heads and enlarge our hearts. In sum, the intent of the Bible is not just to inform us about God but also to involve us in God.

This book hopes to involve the reader with God. With a sensitivity to vocabulary and inclusivity, the first chapter explores language about the sacred scriptures and God. The second is an overview of the names for God found in the Hebrew Scriptures, and is complemented by the third chapter, which explores the variety of human and natural images for God found in the Bible's first half. The fourth chapter wrestles with Jesus and his images for God, while the concluding fifth chapter reflects upon the image of God as Spirit.

Because this book is written for the nonspecialist, no attempt is made to be encyclopedic about every aspect of God purveyed in the texts of the Bible. The modest goal of this book is to acquaint the reader with the myriad of biblical images for God, in the hope that no image will be dismissed or rendered absolute but rather encountered for its worth in developing one's faith.

The reader is encouraged to have a copy of the Bible at hand while reading this book, and to take advantage of the questions for reflection provided at each chapter's end. Additionally, a brief bibliography is provided to stimulate further and wider reading.

I hope this book will help everyone who wrestles with the meaning of God in his or her life and who takes seriously the role of the Bible in developing one's faith. At times, God is as close as one's heartbeat, and at other times as far away as another galaxy, yet always remains the one in whom "we live and move and have our being" (Acts of the Apostles 17:28).

*Soli Deo Gloria*

Jacob got up and took his two wives, his two maids, and his eleven children, and crossed the ford of the Jabbok. He took them and sent them across the stream, and likewise everything he had. Jacob was left alone; and a man wrestled with him until daybreak. When the man saw that he did not prevail against Jacob, he struck him on the hip socket; and Jacob's hip was put out of joint as he wrestled with him. Then he said, "Let me go, for the day is breaking." But Jacob said, "I will not let you go, unless you bless me." So he said to him, "What is your name?" And he said, "Jacob." Then the man said, "You shall no longer be called Jacob, but Israel, for you have striven with God and with humans, and have prevailed." Then Jacob asked him, "Please tell me your name." But he said, "Why is it that you ask my name?" And there he blessed him. So Jacob called the place Peniel, saying, "For I have seen God face to face, and yet my life is preserved." Genesis 32:22–30

# Bible Language and God Language

All scripture is inspired by God.

(2 Timothy 3:16)

**W**hen Christians ask about the right way to speak about God, they look to the Bible as source and inspiration. Before we begin our examination of scripture, we should briefly consider the names and nature of the Christian Bible.

# Chapter One

# Naming Holy Scripture

For Christianity, the Bible is two collections of writings, the Old Testament and the New Testament. Together, they form one scripture whose authority rests equally in both testaments, and not more in one than in the other. In the title *Old Testament*, the word *old* indicates "first," or "what came before," that in which the New Testament is rooted. The English word *testament* is derived from the Greek *diatheke*, meaning "covenant," which is translated into the Latin *testamentum*. For Christians, the new covenant made with Gentiles in Jesus Christ arose from the antecedent covenant God made with Israel. The covenants are interwoven, and this new covenant cannot be properly understood without the first covenant; it does not exist separately.

In light of the problems it raises, the word *old* may not be the best one for naming the first part of the Bible. *Old* can be a neutral word, simply indicating the length of time something has existed, it can connote things and people that are to be especially respected and honored. In current usage, however, *old* often indicates that which is useless, which has become superfluous and so may be discarded. Consider, for a moment, to what lengths we go to avoid using the word *old* when speaking of people. Instead, we prefer words such as *elder, senior* or *retired* when referring to old people.

There is another reason to choose an alternative term: Christians often ignore the fact that the Old Testament is the entire scripture for Judaism. Throughout its history, Christianity's attitude and behavior toward Judaism and the Jews has been painful and shameful, marked by ignorance, blame and persecution. Christianity has often ignored the fact that the first covenant was not canceled by God but that it continues in the postbiblical religion of Judaism. To recognize the authenticity of the Old Testament as the entire sacred scripture for the faith community of Judaism, it is customary in some Christian circles to refer to this part of Christian scripture as the *Hebrew Scriptures* because the text was written almost entirely in Hebrew. About the term *Old Testament*, John T. Pawlikowski comments:

> The time has come to eliminate the term "Old Testament" from the Christian vocabulary about the Bible. Though admittedly the word "old" can connote "reverence" or "long-standing experience," [when] used in reference to the first part of the Bible it tends to create an attitude that these pre-Christian books are inferior and outdated in their religious outlook when compared with the passages of the New Testament. In such a context, the Hebrew Scriptures appear as a forward to the fullness of faith found in the gospels and epistles and at worst as works motivated by legalism and spiritual shallowness which Christians can ignore without in any way impoverishing their spirituality. Continued use of the term "Old Testament" tends to keep Christians from the realization that the Hebrew Scriptures contain rich spiritual insights vital in their own right. It likewise continues to give credence to the discredited contrast between Christianity as a religion of love with Judaism as a faith perspective marked by cold legalism.[1]

# Hebrew Scriptures

There are clear advantages to what is, for many, a new term. When Christians use the term *Hebrew Scriptures*, we stand in humble recognition of and gratitude for our share in the gifts originally intended for those "born in Zion." We recognize that this collection is still the whole of Sacred Scripture for Judaism. In naming the Old Testament as the *Hebrew Scriptures*, the Christian community repents for a past in which it denied authenticity to both the book and the Jews, the people of the book. This repentance is a relevant beginning to our inquiry. Repentance and desire for renewed and healed relations between the Jewish and Christian communities are entirely within the realm of a concern for interreligious dialogue and human dignity. As a term, *Hebrew Scriptures* has the advantage of helping us understand the distance between that biblical text and ourselves. Distance may not sound like an advantage until we consider its implications. The text of the Hebrew Scriptures was composed by and for the faith community of ancient Israel. When Christians direct their attention to this part of the Bible, they tap sources that were not directly created by or for the church.

When we look to the Hebrew Scriptures for responses to our questions about the right way to speak of God, we need to be aware, first of all, that there is a distance between scripture and ourselves. To understand the text and engage it productively with our questions, we must know what was happening in the first covenant community, ancient Israel. We need to know about that community's life, its concerns, and what was happening in that time. Because the languages in which the Bible was written are different from our own, we also ask about words and their meanings in the original languages. Sometimes, we are uncertain of our answers; yet always we must ask the questions. If we begin by admitting to the distance between the Bible and ourselves, then we are at a good starting point for exploration.

There is distance and discontinuity between scripture and ourselves, yet we may also assume closeness and continuity. When we ask how the community of the past spoke about God, and thus how they viewed their own identity and understood divine directives for their life, we also ask about our own naming of the Most Holy One, about our identity, and about God's direction for our lives. In Jesus, those outside Israel are embraced by the love of the God of Israel. Out of Christian engagement with scripture, out of the urgent and honest questions we put to the texts, new understandings of God and of ourselves may emerge. This also applies to the New Testament.

The Bible as a source and inspiration for reflection about God is more than a text reflecting human experience; it is a whole greater than the sum of its parts. There we hope to find God's word for our time, which is no less a time of challenge and crisis than was the time of the birth and rebirth of the ancient covenant community. For that word, we search story and song, prophecy and proverb, and sermon and parable. We look with interest, eagerness and hope, because we wholeheartedly believe that God is not only above all, beyond all, and in all, but is also a living and loving God.

# The Mystery of God and Holy Scripture

The most important reason for reading from, studying with and praying in and through the Bible is its ability to awaken in us a sense of God's presence. Because of this, it is best to hear the scriptures read aloud, as we do in the liturgy. That way, the emotional narrative power of the book comes across most clearly, in what might be called an "Aha!" experience, a sudden insight provoked by the attraction the biblical text exerts upon us. Faith is awakened, and love for God and our fellow humans kindled. We discern the holy mystery in the biblical text as a sudden discovery and are assured of God's presence in our world. It is in proclamation that the holy scripture's power to disclose God's presence and call us to faith is most evident. This is the heart of the Bible's function, if not its only purpose.

Yet the Bible is a very special "product." It defines the Judeo-Christian point of view and, above all, has symbolic power second only to the person of the Lord himself. For Christians, the Bible is not the Word of God; that is Christ. The Bible is the uniquely inspired record of that Word, the product of the Christian community in which the Holy Spirit works to lead us to the truth of God revealed in Christ.

The term *inspired record* should not be understood as mere testimony about past events to which God gives us special insight. The reading or hearing of the scriptures can and should be a means of leading us into the presence of the mystery of God. These writings draw us to knowledge of God in Christ, call us to faith, and hold us accountable to the Lord of all history.

# The Limitation of Human Language

Every person must wrestle at some time with the question of God. Through others, we come to the knowledge and experience of God. The invisible God is rendered visible through other people. We come to know God's love and mercy, justice, compassion and forgiveness through the love, mercy, justice, compassion and forgiveness we receive from and share with others. With infinite wisdom, mercy and patience, God gives us all opportunities to find God on our paths in life.

Yet whenever we reflect upon our experience of God, we face the limitations of language. The English word *theology* comes from two Greek words: *theos*, meaning God, and *logia*, meaning words; therefore, theology literally is "words about God." But words about God are not God!

## Metaphor

When trying to describe God, "we see in a mirror, dimly" (1 Corinthians 13:12), and perceive that God's eternal power and divinity (cf. Romans 1:20) transcend the descriptive powers of human language. For example, whenever we use a metaphor, we use only some of the qualities of the things compared. When I say, "My love is like a rose," I refer to the parts of the rose that are beautiful and delicate, precious and fragrant. I do not mean that the one I love has a long, thorny, green stem in place of legs. This metaphor, like all comparisons, selects parts of a given reality while ignoring others to make its point.

The diverse of images and metaphors for God contained in the Bible both reveal and conceal. For example, the sacred scriptures frequently refer to God as a rock: "The Lord lives! Blessed be my rock" (Psalm 18:46). The attributes of a rock that the psalmist draws upon are its sturdiness, its strength and its everlasting presence. Yet the psalmist does not imply that God is unthinking and insensible, or as unresponsive as a stone. Alternatively, when God is described as an eagle bearing the Israelites out of Egypt (Exodus 19:4), the writer extols the eagle's strength in bearing its young. The author does not mean that God is a bird of prey. The same is true when the psalmist sings "The Lord is my shepherd" (Psalm 23:1). A shepherd's care of a flock is compared to God's care for us; the psalmist does not mean that God's people are dumb sheep.

Similarly, when we address God as Father, we indicate that God, originator of all that exists, loves us as a father loves his children. In using the name Father, we do not imply that God is masculine and married, or that God is authoritarian, possessive and macho or any other negative stereotype. Neither do we imply that God is Father as opposed to being Mother. The Sacred Scripture offers us both images (Matthew 6:9; Luke 11:2; and Isaiah 42:14; 49:15).

A metaphor is only effective if we have knowledge and experience of the things compared. For example, if a person has never seen a rose, the expression "My love is like a rose" would not communicate what it does to someone who knows and enjoys roses. Similarly, when we call God Shepherd, the metaphor communicates a meaning relative to our personal experiences of shepherds, an experience few city-dwellers have. As a result, the metaphor of God as shepherd has no significant meaning for many people. That does not imply that God has no meaning for them, only that this particular metaphor for God has no meaning.

People who have suffered negative experiences of fatherhood have often expressed how difficult it is for them to address God as "Father." Through their human vulnerability parents can distort the ideals of fatherhood and motherhood. Such distortions do not disfigure God because God transcends all metaphors used to express divinity. God is neither father nor mother, nor man nor woman. God is God.

## Always More

All human language about God is inadequate. When either the Sacred Scriptures or we speak about God, we immediately face this limitation. God is a mystery. Words cannot express all that God is. The fact: *Deus est semper major*, "God is always more." All language about and images for God, even those in Sacred Scripture, are just human expressions. They do not define God, rather they articulate some meanings and activities of God. Therefore, all God language is necessarily metaphoric, the language of "as if." Keeping this in mind, we need to be careful to not believe or worship the human words about God, but rather the deity revealed through them. As the *Catechism of the Catholic Church* says:

We must therefore continually purify our language of everything in it that is limited, image-bound or imperfect, if we are not to confuse our image of God—"the inexpressible, the incomprehensible, the invisible, the ungraspable"—with our human representation. Our human words always fall short of the mystery of God.[2]

When we approach the sacred scriptures, we do not worship the words in the book. They are only envelopes carrying images of God. All biblical images for God are lenses through which we gain some sight of God. No one lens, no one image is God. Each provides only one view or angle of vision. Each image must be held in a healthy tension with others. No one image can become absolute or else that image will become an idol. The Bible provides us with a multifaceted approach to God, reflecting many colors in many directions.

## Humility and Awe

It is helpful to develop a posture of humility and awe before all the images of God we encounter in exploring the sacred scriptures. As scholar Elizabeth A. Johnson reminds us, "God dwells in unapproachable light so that no name or image or concept that human beings use to speak of the divine mystery ever arrives at its goal: God is essentially incomprehensible."[3] The reality of God is always greater than our finite concepts and propositions.

Respect for the limitations of language about God and our need to develop a posture of awe are summed up in this reflection:

I can say nothing of God except that I saw the red flames of a cardinal against the snow this morning as I drank tea.

I can say nothing of God except the warm smell of potato soup and the sharp tang of cheddar cheese shimmied up my nose when a friend made lunch for me.

I can say nothing of God except that in the afternoon I washed my face in a cold mountain stream, and it stung my skin and left me feeling fresh and clean.

I can say nothing of God except that two nights ago a cricket sang a funny song in my closet amidst the socks and silence.

I can say nothing of God except that stones can speak, and deer fly in my dreams, that a strange child smiled at me in the supermarket, and that each blade of green grass wears a locket with God's face inside, and that on every hair of my cat's face is written "Alleluia!"

I can say nothing of God except that the rough texture of grainy bread on my tongue and the sweet, liquid acid of grape in my throat are a bitter-sweet memory of compassion and a taste of heaven.[4]

# Inclusive Language and God

Corollary to understanding the metaphoric nature of language about God is the need to avoid all language that excludes any positive reality as an expression of some aspect of God. In this age in particular, we in the church must avoid sexist language, just as we avoid racist language. A healthy Christian spirituality has always been based in community, in the body of believers where there is neither Jew nor Greek, slave nor free person, male nor female (Galatians 3:28). Christian spiritual inclusivity is firmly grounded in the sacred scriptures. Every time we use sexist language, we are legitimating male domination, which is anti-Christian. For example, we may say: "That's not what we mean. We're just referring to humans as 'men' and God as 'he' because it's easier, more practical." In fact, we are really saying that the existence of a male-dominated world is legitimate.

One of the most revolutionary things we can do as faithful Christians is to change language. When Americans of African ancestry said: "We're not Negroes, we're Blacks," the white establishment's initial response was, "Blacks or Negroes, what's the difference? They mean the same thing. *Negro* is simply 'black' in Spanish and Portuguese." Nevertheless, black Americans said, "We'll name ourselves, thank you." Black Americans claimed their own identity, and the whites had to learn to respect that identity. From that respect flowed a change in language.

We have used masculine language and imagery for God in our public life and worship almost exclusively for some 2,000 to 4,000 years. It permeates our imagination. We must open ourselves to the holy mystery of God, a mystery neither male nor female. When we do use gender-specific language, we must balance it as much as possible, and use masculine and feminine images together so that they clash and, in one sense, cancel each other, and, in another sense, enrich each other and yield for us a balanced view of God.

Finally, it is important to understand that language is revelatory. Sexist language reveals patriarchal dominance, while inclusive language reveals community inclusivity and equality. The Bible can be our model because of its inclusive language about and imagery for God.

# For Discussion

1. Why is it important to know how to name the sacred scriptures?

2. Is God a mystery in your life? Please explain.

3. Can you give an example of how human language about God is both limited and inadequate?

4. Do you think sexist language about God should be avoided? Why?

# Names for God in the Hebrew Scriptures

Naming God truthfully is important,
since to name God untruthfully is to delude
ourselves and worship an idol.

Brian Wren[1]

In the ancient Near East, of which Israel was a small part, personal names held great significance, for they revealed character and identity and thus signified existence. To name someone was to enter into a personal relationship. Thus, the revelation of a divine name and its continued use were substantially important to a people as a religious community.

# Chapter Two

The Hebrew Scriptures name God in many ways, a diversity not apparent in most English-language translations. The different names indicate shifts in the experience and perception of God by the covenant community of ancient Israel.

# Elohim

Unlike in the English language, in Hebrew nouns have a gender, as do those of Greek, and many of the world's languages. The Hebrew word *Elohim*—rendered as *God* in English translations of the Hebrew Scriptures—is a plural masculine noun, whose literal meaning is "gods." This is not the most frequently used word for the God of Israel, but it recurs often, and its Greek equivalent *theos* predominates the New Testament. The word *God* may be considered a generic name; it is used in the Bible not only for the God of Israel, the God of Jesus Christ, but also for the deities of other religions. Yet, in the Hebrew Scriptures, *Elohim* names the God of Israel therefore, *God* is not an inaccurate translation since Israel conceived of God as one being, not a plurality of beings.

The verbs coupled to *Elohim*, when used to mean the God of Israel, are most always singular. Thus, Genesis 1:26 announces God's intention to create humanity: "Then God said, 'Let us make humankind in our image, according to our likeness.'" In this verse, God speaks in the plural—"let *us* make *our* image, *our* likeness"—and, in the following lines, the humans created are referred to with the plural pronoun *they*. In the next verse, however, the text backs away from reading plurality in God, reverting to the singular pronoun for God:

> Therefore, God created humankind in his image,
> in the image of God he created them;
> male and female he created them. (Genesis 1:27)

At the announcement of creation in Genesis 1:26, God's speech transcends gender because the first person plural of the verb, the *we* form, is genderless in Hebrew. In verse 27, the pronoun reverts to the masculine singular *he*, but what is created is the plurality, *them*. What is one in God comes out, in the reflection of God, as two differentiated human beings, man and woman.

Genesis 1:27 is uniquely important among all biblical texts where God is the protagonist. It is one of two texts describing the creation of humanity in terms of the image of God (cf. Genesis 4:1–2). Its three lines are constructed as poetry. Hebrew poetry is characterized by repetition and variation of words and phrases and by word order and reversal.

Three important terms are repeated and reordered in this three-line verse: *created, humankind* and *image of God*. The verb *created*, with *God* as its subject, is repeated three times, the first two times in contrasting order. It stands one place from the beginning in line one and one place from the end in line two; threefold repetition, combined with reversal, highlights the action of creation. The Hebrew verb *create* recurs throughout the Bible, but referring only to God's action and never in reference to human acts of shaping or forming. "Humankind,"—*adam* in Hebrew—is repeated at the end of the second and third lines as *them*, while *in his image* recurs as *the image of God* in line two, and a third time as *male and female*.

What does this use of language mean? In Genesis 1, God is in sole charge of creation. God's action is unique, not comparable to human activity because humanity's origin goes back directly to the Creator. *Humanity*, in the first two references, is singular but ends as a plural. This, coupled with the movement from "the image of God" and "his image" to "male and female" could not more clearly state that God's image, a singular one, issues from God in the unique act of creation, and as a plural in humanity. Together and not more in one than in the other, male and female are created in God's image. Biblical scholar Phyllis Trible observes that "Sexual differentiation does not mean hierarchy but equality. Created simultaneously, male and female are not superior and subordinate. Neither has power over the other; in fact, both are given equal power."[2]

Scriptural interpreters carefully point out that the image of God that is humanity may not be read back into God. As Trible observes, "Sexual differentiation of humankind is not thereby a description of God."[3] Does the text then say nothing about God? "Image" and "likeness" are words that may ward off assumptions of identification, but they do point to something or someone.

On the basis of Genesis 1:27, then, what can we say about how we speak of God? According to our textual interpretation, we can say that dignity and equality are guaranteed to men and women. What more can we say? God transcends sexuality and is neither male nor female. Indeed, if God transcends sexuality, as generally inferred from this text, the answer to whether God is male or female is very sophisticated. Based upon Genesis 1:27, one may positively refer to God with feminine and masculine pronouns, with both pronouns equally accurate and inaccurate.

Both feminine and masculine pronouns for God are accurate because they faithfully reflect the original, and, because God is one, human sexual differentiation holds together in God. Feminine and masculine pronouns are equally accurate because sexual difference is non-hierarchical in humanity; as men and women are created equally, they equally reflect God's image. This absence of hierarchy points to the same in God's nature wherein male and female are equal, not one worth more than the other.

At the same time, feminine and masculine pronouns for God remain inaccurate because the image must be distinguished from the original. The existence of two sexes in humanity cannot be read back onto God because God's divinity transcends sexuality. Finally, both male and female pronouns are inaccurate because all speech about God is inaccurate, because people operate within the limitations of language and are always right and always wrong in speaking about God.

Therefore, in Genesis 1:26–27, we find that man and woman are created equally in God's image, and that what does not exist in human hierarchy does not exist in nature's hierarchy: God is not more appropriately named when using either a male or a female designation.

# Eloah and El

*Eloah* and *El* are other words in the Hebrew Scriptures that are translated into the English word *God*. *El* occurs singly and in combinations: *El Elyon* ("God most high," Genesis 14:18–19); *El Olam* ("Eternal God," Genesis 21:33); *El Berith* ("Covenantal God," Judges 9:46) and *El Roi* ("God of seeing" or "God of divination"). Most likely, these names are rooted in the Canaanite religion, in which a deity named *El* headed the pantheon. Outside of Canaan, among Israel's neighbors, *El* was a common name for a deity, and the Hebrew Scriptures use *El* alone or in combination more than 200 times. Yet English translations commonly obscure the multiple forms that underlie the translation of *El* into the word *God*.

# El Shaddai

The name *El Shaddai* is particularly interesting because of its possible implications. Traditionally, this word combination is translated as "God Almighty" (e.g., Exodus 6:3) as in the *New Revised Standard Version* (NRSV) of the Bible, which also gives a note on the Hebrew original. More commonly, this name is given as the single

word *Shaddai,* which is rendered as "Almighty" in the NRSV (e.g., Genesis 49:25), also with a notation about the Hebrew derivation. Thirty-one of the 48 occurrences of *Shaddai* are in the book of Job, with others found in texts as ancient as Genesis 17:1; 49:25, Numbers 24:16, and Psalm 68:14.

The English word *almighty* is derived from the Greek *pantokrator,* a translation of the Hebrew original, and gives only one possible meaning and derivation of *El Shaddai*. Often, scholars translate it as "God of the Mountaintops" or as "God of the Exalted Places." The likeliest grammatical derivation of *Shaddai,* though, is from *shad,* the Hebrew word for breast, which usually occurs as the plural *shaddayim.* Thus, literal translations of *El Shaddai* may be "God of the Breasts" or "The Breasted God." Its connotations of fertility and offspring are clear in Genesis 49:25, and also in the book of Ruth, wherein Naomi complains that God has returned her to Bethlehem "empty" and accuses Shaddai of having done her injury (Ruth 1:22). So interpreted, the names *El Shaddai* or *Shaddai* have obvious female connotations, a connection obscured by the Greek translators of the Hebrew Scriptures, as well as most subsequent translators and interpreters. To maintain an image of male strength, however, those who translated the scriptures into Greek suppressed any feminine roots and meanings for *El Shaddai* by using the Greek masculine noun *pantokrator,* a male image.

Although it may at first feel strange and unfamiliar, Shaddai is perhaps best left untranslated. An entire sentence is best suited to describe this name: "The deity is the source of nutrition and life for the newborn person and for the community of faith." Thus, ancient Israel would see a nursing mother as but one of the many images for God.

# The Holy One of Israel

That God is both unknowable and unnameable may be summarized with the word *holiness*. The Hebrew word for holy, *kadosh*, means "to be cut off from the secular," "to be set apart," "to be singularly unique or different," and "to be totally other." The word *holy* is sometimes used as an adjective modifying the noun *God*, but it can also be translated into the phrase "the Holy One." In that case, the expression comes close to being a name.

Holiness is a complex concept about which volumes have been written. It is helpful to begin with a description by biblical scholar Baruch Levine:

> Holiness is difficult to define or describe, it is a mysterious quality. Of what does holiness consist? In the simplest terms, the "holy" is different from the profane or the ordinary. It is "other" . . . The "holy" is also powerful or numinous. The presence of holiness may inspire awe or strike fear, evoke amazement. The holy may be perceived as dangerous, yet it is urgently desired because it affords blessing, power and protection.[4]

In connection with God, the word *holy* means the otherness of God. In ancient Israel, the quality of otherness was frequently occasion for praise (e.g., Exodus 15:11; Psalms 77:13; 89:7; 99; 111; 9), an example of which is the proclamation of the seraphim in Isaiah's vision:

> Holy, holy, holy is the Lord of Hosts;
> The whole earth is full of his glory. (Isaiah 6:3)

Typically, contemplation of God's holiness provokes both adoration and consideration of human shortcomings in the face of God's splendid perfection. Isaiah therefore cries out that both he and his people are unclean (Isaiah 6:5). The perception and awareness of human flaw evokes fear and awe in the face of God's holiness.

So, if God is other, is God unreachable and aloof? For the Israelites, God was the Holy One, but this did not mean that God was remote. Rather, it emphasized God's uniqueness, that God was unlike any other deity. God was with the people precisely as the Holy One, as the prophet Hosea announces in God's behalf:

> For I am God and no mortal,
>     the Holy One in your midst,
>     and I will not come in wrath. (Hosea 11:9)

This quotation points out two facts about God's holiness: first, God is not a human being (though the Hebrew text reads "a man"); second, it is precisely as the "other" that God is in the midst of the people. Note that in the quotation from Hosea, the likeness between God and human beings is in the quality of forgiveness.

In the book of Isaiah, God is called not just the Holy One, but the Holy One of Israel (Isaiah 1:4; 5:19; 10:17; 12:6; 17:7; 29:19; 30:11–12; 31:1; 37:23; 40:25; 41:14; 43:3; 45:11; 47:4; 48:17; 49:7; 54:5; 55:5; 60:9). As the unknowable Holy Mystery, God is known in Israel and through Israel. For the Christian community, this name focuses attention upon not only God and God's holiness but also upon the Israelites as the holy people of God. We gratefully acknowledge our debt to God and to the Jewish people past and present, God's people.

God's holiness directly relates to the community. Because the Holy One is in our midst, God's holiness is a call. The covenant community created at Mount Sinai was termed a "holy nation" (Exodus 19:6). The most familiar statement may be Leviticus 19:2: "You shall be holy, for I, the Lord your God, am holy." According to Levine, God's holiness is not intended to describe God's essential nature but rather how God is manifest. In Hosea 11:9, God's holiness resides in divine forgiveness. As Levine says: "The statement that God is holy means . . . that God acts in holy ways; God is just and righteous."[5] This insight helps overcome the distinctions interpreters often make between holiness in worship and holiness in the social sphere. Leviticus 19, which is presumed to be centered on liturgical and priestly concerns, contains an entire ethical code. In it we find the commandment to love one's neighbor as one loves oneself (Leviticus 19:18) and to love the stranger in the same way (19:34).

If God's holiness primarily means that God acts justly and righteously, then the community in covenant with God is required to act likewise in following its call to holiness. Thus, the Israelites, as a holy community, are required to be "other" (as God is "other"), to be extraordinary. This quality is most manifest when the community emulates God's passion for justice. Above all other convictions, the Israelite prophets articulated that worship, however constant and devoted, is unacceptable to God when justice is absent from the community's life (cf. Isaiah 1). The naming of God and our concern for justice must be all of a piece: "For the Lord is a God of justice; blessed are all those who wait for him" (Isaiah 30:18).

Justice is always specific in the Hebrew Scriptures; it is God's concern for the downtrodden, those pushed to the margins and squeezed out of society. The covenant community should be holy and apart in its passionate embrace of justice. It should be unlike the rest of the world, which steps on the wounded and further victimizes those already on their way down. In imitation of the Holy One it worships, this community shall not quench the smoldering wick, and the bruised reed it shall not break (cf. Isaiah 42:3). When this passionate love for the poor in society's margins is evident in the community, they will have a sense of what it means to claim the Holy One of Israel as the One it worships.

The terms *Holy One* and *Holy One of Israel* provide something of a transition between a name and a title for God. This naming highlights the connection between language about God and human identity. While the holiness of God points to divine otherness, it also lays claim upon humanity, amid whom God is present as the Holy One. God's holiness calls the community that names God holy to mirror God's justice and righteousness by caring for the most vulnerable. Only then will they be considered holy.

# YHWH

YHWH is the most important of God's names in the Hebrew Scriptures; it is a tetragrammaton ("four letters") that occurs more than 6,000 times throughout the Bible. Though usually pronounced "Yahweh," its true pronunciation was lost ages ago. Because of the sanctity attached to this name and the consequent desire to avoid its misuse, the Hebrew title *Adonai*, "My Great Lord," was pronounced in place of the tetragrammaton. When written, the vowels of *Adonai* were combined with the consonants YHWH, reminding readers to utter *"Adonai"* instead of the sacred name. This sanctity of God's personal name is still honored in contemporary Judaism.

In the third chapter of Exodus, the name YHWH is revealed to Moses at the burning bush on Mount Horeb. A profound exchange about God's name occurs between God and Moses, when he is appointed leader of the Israelites and charged with freeing them from Egyptian slavery. Once commissioned, he asks God's name:

> But Moses said to God, "If I come to the Israelites and say to them, 'The God of your ancestors has sent me to you,' and they ask me, 'What is his name?' what shall I say to them?" God said to Moses, "I am who I am." [or "I am what I am" or "I will be what I will be"]. He said further, "Thus you shall say to the Israelites, 'I am has sent me to you.'" (Exodus 3:13–14)

Representing ancient Israel, Moses asked and was answered. The answer he received may have been unsatisfactory, for it was a partial answer. After all, he asked for God's name. God's response to Moses is both enigma and revelation; it simultaneously safeguards the freedom of God "to be" in accordance with God's nature, and the guarantee to be present according to divine promise.

Exodus 3:14 reveals certain things about God. First, God promised to be present in the world with the Israelites, God's people. That promise stands. It has the weight of God's word behind it. It is up to Moses, to the people of Israel and to us to live faithfully with that truth. Second, God's presence may be counted on, though its manner is unpredictable. God will be present as God wills, not as dictated by history or religion or sacred texts.

The community's identity is bound up in God's identity. God goes forward into the wilderness with the escaped slaves; out there they will discover the one God and themselves. In the wilds, they will find themselves transformed as a people into a new and better community by the God who promises a continuing presence in their community. Like the community's, Moses' identity is bound up with God's. Thus, when Moses asks: "Who are you?" and "What is your name?" he simultaneously asks: "Who am I, what is my identity?" These same questions are repeated by the Israelites, the people led and represented by Moses.

Moses is in trouble, for being in God's presence is awesome but manageable as long as he knows where he stands. He thought he knew enough about the God of his ancestors to handle being in the divine presence. Now, before the burning bush, his old definitions crumble as he gropes in a fog to understand. Therefore, he asks a sincere question of God—ostensibly for a name. In reply, Moses is told: "I will be who I will be," more and less than a name.

## The Enigmatic Name for God

This name appears as three words in Hebrew: *ehyeh asher ehyeh*. The Septuagint, the Greek translation of the Hebrew Scriptures, interprets the name as "I am who I am." Ordinarily, these Hebrew verb forms would be translated into the future tense: "I will be" rather than "I am." There is a long tradition in both Judaism and Christianity that understands that this phrase speaks to the unchangeable, mysterious nature of God's being.

Commenting on Exodus 3:14, the Jewish scholar Martin Buber notes that *asher*, the Hebrew word for "that" also means "whatever." In other words, God's earliest self-revelation to Moses implies that God will not be limited to any specific revelation but "will be whatever God wishes to be."[6]

In Hebrew, the verb *to be* does not "carry a meaning of pure existence. It means happening, coming into being, being there, being present, being thus and thus, but not the abstract sense of being."[7] It appears, then, that Greek grammar and philosophy influenced this translation in a looser direction unintended in the original Hebrew, an influence readily acceptable in the world of the early church. In Hebrew language and thought, God's being is spoken of as God relates to creation. Apart from this revelation, consideration of God's being is of no interest to the writers of the Hebrew Scriptures. The statement "I will be who I will be" (Exodus 3:14) is about God's being and about God's relating. To divide these two states creates a too narrow understanding of what the text attempts to convey. What is contained in these three Hebrew words about God?

To begin, the answer Moses receives does not provide a name at all, and so it is impossible to speak about or to pray to God by name. Despite such ambiguity, this is the only place in the Bible where God is named. Is God toying with Moses, teasing him? Or does "I will be who I will be" indicate annoyance, even anger, that Moses dares ask such a question? It is impossible to be certain, but one can assume that the answer to "What is your name?" is a profoundly serious one that responds to the question on different levels. The cryptic phrase-name says what it means, and means what it says: "I will be who I will be." Given that it is impossible to name God, speaking of God begins with recognizing that impossibility and progressing toward that same insight and understanding. In the end, YHWH[8] is unpronounceable.

Moses reaches an important theological juncture: The mystery of God cannot be captured in a name. For Moses, that knowledge was a good beginning, and it is a good beginning for us. As we recognize the impossibility of naming God, we recognize our need to do so. In Exodus 3, the statement "I will be who I will be" is surrounded by names for God. *God* occurs (3:1 and throughout), as well as "God of the ancestors" (3:6, 13, 15, 16); above all one finds *YHWH*. The search for the proper way to speak about God, and to God, does not occur in a vacuum.

## A Name That Promises God's Presence

In Exodus 3:14, the name that is not a name holds both a denial and an affirmation. Buber eloquently translates the phrase as: "I will be present as I will be present."[9] John Courtney Murray puts it: "I shall be there as who I am shall I be there."[10] In effect, God is saying: "The manner of my being present is as I will it, not to be caught in one image or manipulated by one name. But I will be present. I was present in the past, I am present now, and I will be in your future." The God of scripture, the God of Jesus Christ promises presence above all. It is in this presence and because of it that our transformed existence becomes a possibility.

The Israelites had a long way to travel from enslavement by the Egyptians to freedom, from being a motley crowd to becoming a community. First they had to face their enslavement and recognize it for the bondage it was. Then they had to bid it farewell. Often, bonds, though painful, may feel familiar and so be more difficult to break than one had supposed. One thing was certain: Without God's presence and the vision it provided they would not become free.

We, too, have a long way to go. Our enslavement to oppressive ways of being and acting must be recognized as destructive so that we may break them and bid them farewell, and progress to freedom. We all face a long trek in the wilderness, where old, familiar behaviors will have to disappear. Though oppressive, we may cling to them, just as Israel once clung to the fleshpots of Egypt. One thing is certain: Without God's presence and our mindfulness of it, we will not become free.

The people freed from slavery in Egypt had to learn new ways of being together so that they could become a community that mirrored God's passionate and loving justice. God, as eagle, has borne them out of Egypt on strong wings and into the wilderness, ready to let them try their wings, like an anxious parent ready to let go of a child. Yet, as the Israelites moved into a new existence, they were accompanied by God's presence, "a shelter to them by day, and a starry flame through the night" (Wisdom 10:17).

## The God of the Future

When *ehyeh asher ehyeh* (Exodus 3:14) is translated as "I am who I am," its most important aspect, lost in translation, is the dynamism of revelation about God, and its openness to the future. For this reason, Murray translates the phrase as "I shall be there as who I am shall I be there."[11]

Like Moses, we may recognize that God is anchored in past promises. This is expressed in the title "the God of your ancestors" (Exodus 3:15, 16; 4:5). This acknowledgment is important because the ancient covenant community of Israel constantly reflected upon the presence of God in its history.[12] In story and song, as well as in prayer and precept, they articulated the conviction that God had always been the God of their deliverance. Looking to the past, ancient Israel constantly renewed its trust in God's continually liberating presence. In so doing, they recaptured and reshaped old images of God. When Second Isaiah reimagined God the manly warrior as a woman in childbirth, past and present images were woven together, signaling new possibilities for the future in God's presence (Isaiah 42:13–14).

We, too, look to the past, to the history of God with Israel and the world as reflected in the Bible. It can be seductive, however, to look for God only in the past, locking God in old images. "I will be who I will be" also means that the manner of God's presence in the community and the world is to be named anew, again and again, as the community's experience changes and God's presence needs to be reimagined. "I will be who I will be" means that God is to be spoken about in the past, the present and the future tenses, so that discussion about God is never closed. Of course, the past and the present will always guide and inform such discussion. Moreover, the biblical text awaits our new questions and interpretations, so that God's word can come into being for our time.

Many years ago, when my daughter, Laura, was eight years old, she reminded me that discussion about God could never be closed. When asked about her understanding of God, she replied: "God does not have any edges. God is inside me, but if you cut me open, you won't find him there because he is too big." God exceeds our designations and wildest imaginings, so much so that the Bible and its naming of God cannot contain the wondrous mystery of who God is.

## For Discussion

1. What does a name convey to you?

2. Is being able to name God important for you?

3. What connotations and denotations do you have about "I am who I am?"

4. What are some of the names you apply to God? Do you have a favorite one?

# Images for God in the Hebrew Scriptures

Prepare to meet your God, O Israel!

(Amos 4:12)

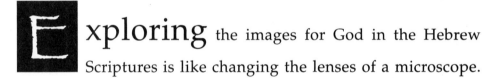

**E**xploring the images for God in the Hebrew Scriptures is like changing the lenses of a microscope. What is on the slide—in this case, the mystery of God—remains unchanged; what changes is the lens used to observe. Biblical writers knew and understood that the divine mystery is beyond human comprehension, and so understood that whatever lens is used or the image it produced was but a perception of God and not the reality of God.

# Chapter Three

The writers of the Bible know that all knowledge of God is indirect. Moses is not permitted to see God's face (Exodus 33:23). Isaiah sees God enthroned but describes only the skirts of God's robe (Isaiah 6:1), whereas Isaiah 31:3 implies that God is by nature not flesh but spirit. Ezekiel sees a human form glowing from the waist up and radiating fire from the waist down. Of that, Ezekiel says, it "was the appearance of likeness of the glory of the Lord" (Ezekiel 1:27–28).

The writers of the Bible are more comfortable with imagery than with definitions, but even their attempts only describe the distance between the human and the divine. God does not vacillate as human beings do (1 Samuel 15:29). Human judges may be corruptible (e.g., 1 Samuel 8:3), but the judge of all the earth is just (Genesis 18:25). God's love is everlasting (Psalm 100:5), even though Israel's love evaporates like the morning mist (Hosea 6:4).

Having observed this distance between the human and the divine, the writers nonetheless draw upon a variety of human experiences in depicting God's nature and action. From experience of the natural and the animal worlds come such animate and inanimate images of God as the sun (Psalm 84:11), as a thundering torrent or a mighty voice (Exodus 19:19), as one whose spirit is like the wind (Genesis 1:1–2) and whose justice and wisdom are like an irrigating river. God is also a rock (Psalm 18:3, 32, 47), a spring, a shield (Psalm 3:4), a fortress (Psalms 18:3; 31:4; 91:2) and a devouring fire. Furthermore, God is territorial and tenacious in defending offspring as are the panther, the lion, the leopard or the bear (Hosea 13:8). When depicted as a human being, God is a potter, a builder, a farmer, a shepherd, a hero, a warrior, a doctor, a judge, a midwife, a bird catcher, a woman in labor, a king, a husband and a father, all images of people protective of their community. God is said to have a head, face, eyes, eyelids, ears, nostrils, mouth, voice, arm, hand, palm, fingers, foot, heart, bosom and bowels. Yet despite these natural, animal and human images, God in the Hebrew Scriptures remains the one God.

The most important aspect of the Israelite religion is its expectation that as a people they were to worship only the one true God. All other gods were false and powerless; only the God of ancient Israel was true and alive. The *Sh'ma* is the fundamental expression of this faith.

> Hear, O Israel: The Lord is our God, the Lord alone. You shall love the Lord your God with all your heart, and with all your soul, and with all your might. (Deuteronomy 6:4–5)

Despite this expectation, biblical history is replete with sad episodes of the Israelites' infidelity to God, such as their continual reversion to the worship of false gods. Nevertheless, the Hebrew Scriptures also tell the happy story of God's continuous, loving faithfulness despite the forgetful infidelity of the chosen people.

The Israelites evolved into monotheists, believers in and worshipers of only one God. This God is seen to be eternal (Deuteronomy 33:27), powerful (Psalm 29:4), the creator of heaven and earth (Genesis 1—3; Isaiah 40:28), the holy one who forms a holy people (Isaiah 6:3; 57:15; Leviticus 11:54), savior (Psalm 27:1;

Isaiah 43:3), compassionate and merciful (Exodus 34:6–7), who stands in judgment over idolatrous human arrogance (Isaiah 2:8–10; 45:18–25).

# Titles for God

The political matrix in which ancient Israel and its contemporary Near Eastern cultures existed provided a host of titles and images for God. Among the more important are king (Psalm 95:3), judge (Genesis 18:25) and shepherd (Psalm 23). The first and second signify God's rule over Israel, while the last signifies the loving care of God.

For many people today, the image of the shepherd needs explaining. There is a close bond between shepherd and sheep. A shepherd knows each sheep's characteristics and idiosyncrasies, and counts them often to ensure none has strayed from the flock. As for the sheep, they recognize and follow only the familiar voice of their shepherd. Since shepherds spent so much time alone with the sheep, they often talk to them and look upon them as companions. This pastoral metaphor is masterfully portrayed in Psalm 23:

The Lord is my shepherd, I shall not want.
  He makes me lie down in green pastures;
he leads me beside still waters;
  he restores my soul.
He leads me in right paths
  for his name's sake.

Even though I walk through the darkest valley,
  I fear no evil;
for you are with me;
  your rod and your staff—
  they comfort me.

You prepare a table before me
  in the presence of my enemies;
you anoint my head with oil;
  my cup overflows.

Surely, goodness and mercy shall follow me
  all the days of my life,
and I shall dwell in the house of the Lord
  my whole life long.

Through the prophet Ezekiel, God expresses profound grief over the neglectfulness of the Israelites; they were scattered over the face of the earth with no one to look after them (Ezekiel 34:5–6). "You are my sheep," God declares tenderly, "and I am your God" (Ezekiel 34:31). The prophet Isaiah also uses this image: "He will feed his flock like a shepherd; he will gather the lambs in his arms, and carry them in his bosom, and gently lead the mother sheep" (Isaiah 40:11).

Contrary to the false impression many people have, God never abandons us but always seeks us out and draws us back should we stray or purposely turn against God:

> For thus says the Lord God: "I myself will search for my sheep, and will seek them out. As shepherds seek out their flocks when they are among their scattered sheep, so I will seek out my sheep. I will rescue them from all the places to which they have been scattered on a day of clouds and thick darkness." (Ezekiel 34:11–12)

 The shepherd is one of many title images for God used by Jesus (cf. Matthew 18:12–14; Luke 15:4–7; John 10:14–15 and 28). Other important titles are derived from the Israelite family structure, lord/father (Deuteronomy 32:6); brother *(Ahijah,* "brother of YHWH" in Hebrew, 1 Samuel 14:3); kinsman (or "the fear of Isaac" in Genesis 31:42); and redeemer (Psalm 19:14). These patriarchal titles originated in a religion in which the patriarch's personal deity is protector of the group: "I am the God of your father." (Exodus 3:6).

Tribes were held together with blood ties, direct and indirect, creating communal solidarity and mutual obligation to help and protect one another. In the Israelite community, this obligation was realized in the office of *go'el,* Hebrew for "redeemer" and "recoverer." As next of kin, he had the duty to safeguard the life and integrity of the tribe in general and the family in particular. Thus, if property were lost, the *go'el* should buy it back (Leviticus 25:25; Jeremiah 32:6–7), and if anyone were sold into slavery, the *go'el* should free him or her (Leviticus 25:47–49). If a tribesman dies childless, the *go'el* should, as *levir,* brother-in-law, beget children with the widow so that the dead man's lineage, honor and inheritance persevere (this is "Levirate Law"; cf. Deuteronomy 25:5–10; Genesis 38:8; Ruth 2:20; 3:12; 4:4).

How is God the *go'el* for the Israelites? It means that Israel and God formed one family, and as a faithful member of the family, God assumed the role of *go'el* and redeemed the Israelites from their Egyptian slavery. This profound recognition of kinship with God is expressed in the rituals sealing the covenant (Exodus 24): "Moses sprinkled the blood on the altar, representing God, and then on the people. They have the same blood 'in their veins'; they are family. Those who choose to be part of God's family have the same blood type as God."[1]

# What Kind of Being Is the God of the Hebrew Scriptures?

In the Hebrew Scriptures, God is revealed as both transcendent and immanent. The prophet Isaiah masterfully describes God's transcendence as entirely other than creation: "For my thoughts are not your thoughts, nor are your ways my ways, says the Lord" (Isaiah 55:8). In Genesis, God's immanence is described: "They heard the sound of the Lord God walking in the garden at the time of the evening breeze" (Genesis 3:8).

The Hebrew Scriptures and the faith of ancient Israel hold in balance God's transcendence and immanence, thus seeking to avoid the extremes of either removing God entirely from the world or making God too mundane, thereby limiting divinity. Several scripture passages help us learn of divine transcendence and immanence.

## Transcendence

*God is eternal:* "Have you not known? Have you not heard? The Lord is the everlasting God, the creator of the ends of the earth. He does not faint or grow weary; his understanding is unsearchable" (Isaiah 40:28).

*God is unique:* "I am the Lord, and there is no other" (Isaiah 45:18).

*God is omnipotent:* "For I know the Lord is great; our Lord is above all gods. Whatever the Lord pleases he does, in heaven and on earth, in the seas and all deeps" (Psalm 135:5–6).

*God is immense:* This is beautifully voiced by King Solomon's prayer at the dedication of the temple: "But will God indeed dwell on the earth? Even heaven and the highest heaven cannot contain you, much less this house that I have built!" (1 Kings 8:27).

*God contains all things:* This is especially portrayed in the book of Wisdom, where Lady Wisdom and God are synonymous. It is she who "reaches mightily from one end of the earth to the other, and she orders all things well" (Wisdom 8:1).

*God cannot be praised enough:* "Where can we find the strength to praise him? For he is greater than all his works" (Sirach 43:28).

## Immanence

*God cannot be avoided:* "Where can I go from your Spirit? Or where can I flee from your presence? If I ascend to heaven, you are there; if I make my bed in Sheol, you are there. If I take the wings of the morning and settle at the farthest limits of the sea, even there your hand shall lead me, and your right hand shall hold me fast" (Psalm 139:7–10).

*God chooses the Hebrew tribes and makes them a people:* "It was not because you were more numerous than any other people that the Lord set his heart on you—for you were the fewest of all peoples. It was because the Lord loved you and kept the oath that he swore to your ancestors, that the Lord has brought you out with a mighty hand, and redeemed you from the house of slavery, from the hand of Pharaoh king of Egypt" (Deuteronomy 7:7–8).

*God establishes a covenant with God's people:* "The Lord our God made a covenant with us at Horeb. Not with our ancestors did the Lord make this covenant, but with us, who are all of us here alive today" (Deuteronomy 5:2; cf. Genesis 6—9; 15, 17; Exodus 19—24; and Deuteronomy 5—7).

*God frees the Hebrews from Egypt:* "I [God] have come down to deliver them from the Egyptians, and to bring them up out of that land to a good and broad land, a land flowing with milk and honey." (Exodus 3:8).

*God gives the people of Israel a land:* Under Joshua's leadership, the people take possession of the land. God tells Joshua, "Pass through the camp and command the people: Prepare your provisions; for in three days you are to cross over the Jordan, to go in to take possession of the land that the Lord your God gives you to possess" (Joshua 1:11).

*God sends prophets to guide and sustain the people:* In the Hebrew Scriptures, revelation is grounded in the conviction that "surely the Lord God does nothing without revealing his secret to his servants the prophets" (Amos 3:7).

*God sustains the chosen people in Babylon and restores them to Israel:* "Comfort, O comfort my people, says your God. Speak tenderly to Jerusalem, and cry to her that she has served her term, that her penalty is paid, that she has received from the Lord's hand double for all her sins" (Isaiah 40:1–2).

# Inanimate Images for God

Although many of the images in the Hebrew Scriptures are comparisons with animate beings, there are also inanimate images for God. We will explore two of them, the wind and the rock.

## Wind

One ancient Hebrew word for an image of God was *ruach*, "wind," a natural, even impersonal concept. The wind was seen not as a living being but as a boundless, vitalizing force. The wind of God was not eternal; rather, it emerged from the world and was understood as its life-giving reality. In the Bible's creation story, God's *ruach* brooded over chaos in order to bring forth life (Genesis 1:1–12). Slowly, the concept of *ruach* evolved from an impersonal force to the personalized entity, "spirit." This *ruach* was also connected to the *nephesh*, "human breath" in Hebrew, which is a force that wells up from us and is identical with our life.

## Rock

The rock is another inanimate image for God, one of the most celebrated in the Hebrew Scriptures. In the book of Samuel we find the phrase, "There is no rock like our God" (1 Samuel 2:2), while the Psalmist proclaims, "The Lord is my rock, my fortress, and my deliverer" (Psalm 18:2), and later, "Who is a rock besides our God?" (Psalm 18:31). Paul called Jesus Christ the rock from which sprang the water that slaked the Israelites' thirst during their wilderness years (1 Corinthians 10:4).

# Animal Metaphors for God

Given that the Hebrew Scriptures use inanimate images to express immutable aspects of God's nature, it is not surprising that animal images are used to describe the more humanly accessible aspects of God's nature.

## Fierce and Loving

In the book of Hosea, animal imagery of God is presented in this passage:

> I have been the Lord your God
> ever since the land of Egypt;
> you know no God but me,
> and besides me there is no savior.
> It was I who fed you in the wilderness,
> in the land of drought.
> When I fed them, they were satisfied;
> they were satisfied, and their heart was proud;
> therefore they forgot me.
> So I will become like a lion to them,
> like a leopard I will lurk beside the way.
> I will fall upon them like a bear robbed of her cubs,
> and will tear open the covering of their heart;
> there I will devour them like a lion,
> as a wild animal would mangle them. (Hosea 13:4–8)

Hosea draws an image both wild and loving, like an enraged mother bear. Similarly Jeremiah compares God to a fierce lion (See Jeremiah 25:38).

## Eagle

Of all animal images applied to God, none surpasses the eagle: "You have seen what I did to the Egyptians, and how I bore you on eagles' wings and brought you to myself" (Exodus 19:4).

This image of God as an eagle is parental, both protective and educational in nature. The eagle has been a symbol of strength and power since ancient times. Of the 27 times the word *eagle* appears in the Hebrew Scriptures, only twice does it refer to the bird; all other occurrences are figurative. Sometimes an enemy nation is depicted as bearing down on Israel with the speed and strength of an eagle (Deuteronomy 27:48; Jeremiah 4:13; Habakkuk 1:8; Lamentations 4:19). Sometimes, God threatens to fall upon Israel's enemies, "swooping down like an eagle" (Jeremiah 48:40; 49:16, 22 and Obadiah 4). This image emphasizes strength and speed, as when David laments over the deaths of Saul and Jonathan, calling them "swifter than eagles, stronger than lions" (2 Samuel 1:23).

In these passages, the eagle dives on its prey with ferocious speed and singleness of purpose. Its vigor revives the depleted community found in Isaiah

40:31: "They shall mount up with wings like eagles." Compare that to Psalm 103:5: "Your youth is renewed like the eagle's."

Mystery and awe naturally surround such a splendid and powerful creature. The Wisdom writers thus ponder the eagle's "way in the sky" (Proverbs 30:19), while in Ezekiel's visions, one of the four heavenly creatures has the face of an eagle (Ezekiel 1:10). The connotations of swiftness and strength deepen and enrich the image whenever it appears in the Bible. These qualities are especially significant in these two passages, Exodus 19:3–6 and Deuteronomy 32:10–13.

*Exodus 19:3–6:* The first 24 chapters of the book of Exodus divide into two parts. Chapters 1 through 15 tell the sojourn of the Israelites in Egypt, their exodus from that country, and their military victory over Pharaoh at the Sea of Reeds. Chapters 16 through 24 concern the journey to Sinai and the founding there of the covenant between God and the people. Israel understood that it had been set free to live as a community in the presence of God. To shape and define this purpose, they receive divine instructions for their conduct as a community in special relationship with God. This is narrated in Exodus 24, which describes the promises and blood rite that seal the covenant.

From the outset, God commissioned Moses as intermediary, in the roles of priest and prophet. At the beginning of the story of the events at Sinai, Moses is given the great declaration that recounts Israel's past, present and future:

> And Moses went up to God; and the Lord called to him from the mountain, saying, "Thus you shall say to the house of Jacob, and tell the Israelites: You have seen what I did to the Egyptians, and how I bore you on eagles' wings and brought you to myself. Now therefore, if you will obey my voice and keep my covenant, you shall be my treasured possession out of all peoples. Indeed, the whole earth is mine, but you shall be for me a priestly kingdom and a holy nation. These are the words that you shall speak to the Israelites." (Exodus 19:3–6)

God's goal in freeing Israel from slavery and domination is their arrival in God's presence: "I bore you on eagles' wings and brought you to myself." Verse four recounts God's past actions and results; and verses five and six endow the people with both promise and change. It is Israel's great commission to be ever alert for God's voice so that they keep the covenant. If they proceed from this foundation, they have it in themselves to become God's treasured people above all the other nations of earth. All nations are under God's care, but Israel is to be a sign of justice to the world. As a realm of priests dedicated to a life of mutual *shalom*, Israel will mediate with God in behalf of others.

This context is important in order to understand the words about God as eagle. First, there is the image of Egypt, the enslaving nation itself enslaved to pride and ferocity. What fates befell Israel and Egypt are contrasted by implication: Egypt, weighted with ferocious pride, fell to the sea, while Israel rose from bondage. Both actions are ascribed to God: "You have seen what I did to the Egyptians, and how I bore you on eagles' wings and brought you to myself" (Exodus 19:4).

Second, the eagle's wing images have multiple implications: To the strength, speed and ferocity that characterize the image elsewhere in the Bible, the qualities of protection and education are added. The comparison of God to an eagle is parental: Both mother and father train eaglets to fly by example. They rouse the young birds to flight by flapping their wings. When the young are aloft, the parent birds fly under the eaglets, ever ready to catch them should they falter and fall. Analogously, the young, fledgling Israel was stirred out of Egypt and in its immature state was carried out and protected by God.

The people, however, must not remain nestlings forever. Now brought into God's presence, they are ready to receive the charge of adulthood. In God's presence, they must fly under the power of their wings and in the manner God charges. In Exodus 19:3, this parental image of God is one of both protection and preparation, one that does not bind the Israelites into perpetual, childish dependence.

*Deuteronomy 32:10–13* refers to the same period in Israel's history as the Exodus passage that was just examined. The passage from Deuteronomy examines more closely the image of God as an eagle:

> He sustained him in a desert land,
>    in a howling wilderness waste;
> he shielded him, cared for him,
>    guarded him as the apple of his eye.
> As an eagle stirs up its nest,
>    and hovers over its young;
> as it spreads its wings, takes them up,
>    and bears them aloft on its pinions,
> the Lord alone guided him;
>    no foreign god was with him.
> He set him atop the heights of the land,
>    and fed him with produce of the field;
> he nursed him with honey from the crags,
>    with oil from flinty rock. (Deuteronomy 32:10–13)

The inspired author does not limit himself to one symbol of abundant sustenance; he stacks them one atop the other: honey, oil and produce of the field, all are provided. The emphasis on the nature of God's care as providing more than necessary for sustenance sets Israel's rebellion in sharp relief (Exodus 32:15–18).

In this passage, the eagle image is sustained from verse 11 to the beginning of verse 13, where God sets the people of Israel on the heights, as eagles do with eaglets. As already noted the nurturing eagle image is parental rather than either solely paternal or maternal. Deuteronomy 32:13, however, slants the comparison in favor of the maternal and changes image in the middle of verse 13: God is a mother nursing her children.

In the Bible, God's wing is not an uncommon symbol of protection. Wings may be assigned to supernatural beings or to the wind. When assigned to God, the word *wings* is most always accompanied by the word *shadow*. The shadow of God's wings is a guarded place, safe from terror. The believer prays:

> Guard me as the apple of the eye;
>     hide me in the shadow of your wings,
> from the wicked who despoil me,
> my deadly enemies who surround me. (Psalm 17:8–9)

Wings also are familiar features of the supernatural creatures that move between the human and the celestial realms. In the Christian tradition, God's spirit assumes the form of the dove.

The biblical image of God as eagle defends, protects and educates the human community and provides a universal parent image, though circumstances often emphasize its maternal aspect. Humans are recipients of this care but are also at risk by God's stirring up the nest. In the parental comparison embedded in the image of God as a bird, humanity is actively growing up and moving out of the nest, rather than in a static parent and child relationship.

# God the Protagonist

God is the central character in the drama that is the Bible and is the principal speaker throughout the Hebrew Scriptures and the New Testament. We need to remember that scripture does not present God as object—the one acted upon— but as its subject, the protagonist who shares the stage of creation with humanity. From the scriptural perspective, God is the creator, clan leader, friend of the family, liberator and warrior.

## God as Creator

In the opening chapters of Genesis, God is the creator who brings order to chaos and sees all of creation as good, who rests on the seventh day so as not to make slaves of creatures and creation, who makes humanity in the divine image and likeness; who enthrones humanity as king and queen of the animal world, who is in union with creation and gives the original blessing.

The two biblical creation stories tell us that God is creator of the universe and humanity. Our greatest challenge is that we are made in God's image: "So God created humankind in his image, in the image of God he created them; male and female he created them" (Genesis 1:26).

At one time "in the image of God" was understood as a characteristic built into us by God. Theologians then tried to identify this characteristic. Contemporary scholars think that the biblical writers were unlikely to have referred to a divine element within humanity because that would have been out of keeping with

Semitic thought. The Hebrew Scriptures explore the roles people assume and their relationships to others and to things; rarely do they define natures or essences.

What, then, does the phrase "in the image of God" assert about the roles of human beings in creation? The Hebrew Scriptures shed little light on this question since the phrase is infrequently used outside of Genesis 1. Therefore, scholars look in two other directions to learn its meaning.

First, they examine how the phrase "created in the image of God" functions within the structure of Genesis 1. If verses 26 through 28 were not there, Genesis 1 would seem to say that humanity is the highest form of life in God's creative repertoire. As it stands, the phrase "in the image of God" avoids such misinterpretation; verses 26 through 28 set off the creation of humans from the creation of other animals. "Created in the image of God" indicates that humans are much more than the earth's dominant animal.

Second, scholars look for appearances of the phrase "in the image of God" outside the Bible. Studies of the cultures of Mesopotamia and Egypt reveal that "in the image of God" was a term applied to their kings. Thus, "created in the image of God" means we were appointed as kings and queens ruling the earth in God's behalf. This interpretation is supported by Genesis 1:26, "and let them have dominion."

Third, the Semitic outlook viewed the human being as a whole; it did not inquire about the separate concepts of the body and the soul. Thus, Genesis 1:26–28 speaks of our whole being sharing in the dignity of being God's royal representative. Thus, in the biblical view, we resemble God not only physically but also in mind and will.

Fourth, the scholars also note that Genesis 1:26–28 does not speak of the creation of individual human beings. For example, *adam,* the Hebrew word sometimes translated as "man," is used in most scriptural instances as a collective term for humanity. Thus in Genesis 1 it is the human race that God sets apart from the other creatures and appoints as God's earthly regents. The entire human race bears the likeness of God. Individuals share it by membership in the human community.

Therefore, God the creator is best represented by the epitome of creation, humanity—men and women alike.

## God as Friend of the Family or Head of the Clan

In Genesis, each of the patriarchs experiences God in a special way, freely entrusting himself to God. Certain archaic names connote close personal relationships between the clan father and his God: the God of Abraham (28:13); the Fear of Isaac (closer translation than "kinsman") (31:42); the Mighty One of Jacob (49:24). In Genesis 31:36–55, Jacob swears by the Fear of Isaac, and Laban by the God of Nahor, each man swearing his oath before the patronal deity of his clan. This has been called the "God of the Fathers" type of religion, which is further supported by extra-biblical evidence.

Through some religious experience, each patriarch became convinced that the deity who had spoken to him was both his and the clan's god. Therefore, the patriarch's clan was of the patron deity's family because of the solidarity existing between the two. Contained in this view is the idea of election. The patriarch had been chosen by God. Hence, God and the patriarch's clan were joined in covenant. This was made manifest in promises of offspring and land.

One final point worth noting. In general, ancient Near Eastern religions were tied to the seasons of the year. For example, in the Canaanite religion the fertility god, Baal, died in the autumn and returned to life in the spring. The Israelite patriarchal religion was unlike its contemporaries because God was connected to the clan, not to nature. Thus, the God of the Fathers was closely tied to human history.

## God as Liberator

Throughout the book of Exodus, especially in its first 15 chapters, God is the one who liberates Israel from its bondage in Egypt. God challenges and combats the gods of Egypt and their incarnations, the pharaohs. It is God who visits ten plagues upon Egypt and helps the Israelites cross the Red Sea and stands by them during their wanderings in the wilderness. All these were events of liberation.

In the book of Exodus, God frees the Israelites not only from historical Egypt but also from the dominant culture, which Egypt symbolizes. Freed from this slavery, they are now to proclaim the saving activity of their one true God, who liberates all people from cultural oppression. In light of this, the Israelites realized that God was their *go'el*, their redeemer.

## God of the Covenant

Ancient Israel understood itself to be in a covenant with God. This covenant was an agreement between superior and inferior in which both parties agreed to certain obligation and both made promises. God enters into covenant again and again, with Noah and all humanity (Genesis 6–9); with Abraham and Sarah and their descendents, promising the blessings of land and children (Genesis 15 and 17); with Moses and the Israelites, promising to be their God if they will keep covenant (Exodus 19—24; and Deuteronomy 5—7) and with David and his descendants (2 Samuel 7).

On each occasion, God freely chooses to relate to the Israelites with a *berith*, a solemn agreement. Therefore, the *Benai Berith* are the people of the covenant, God's chosen, who are bound as strongly and intimately as are a husband and wife. Unique to this relationship is the fact that God does not default on promises made, regardless of the people's failures to fulfill their promises. Thus, a covenant is the bonding of mortal and immortal, a blood pact that obliges the mortal partners to keep the commandments agreed upon, most especially the commandment to believe in and worship only the one God.

## God as Warrior

One fundamental image of God in the Hebrew Scriptures is that of the warrior (Exodus 15:3; Psalm 24:8; and Isaiah 42:13). Israel's wars were often ideological, emerging from their understanding of God's nature, which makes their enemies the Lord's enemies (Judges 5:31; 1 Samuel 30:26), and the knowledge that the Lord assists Israel in wartime (Exodus 14:13–14; Joshua 10:11; 24:12; 1 Samuel 17:45). Although "holy war" is never mentioned in the Hebrew Scriptures, divinely sanctioned wars are (Joshua 8:1; Judges 4:14–15; 1 Samuel 23:4; 2 Kings 3:18). While divine war is a problem for theologians and ethicists, we must recognize that war was a commonplace cultural activity in the ancient Near East.

Although not every war that Israel fought was interpreted as a religious event, the disastrous defeat that led to the Babylonian Exile in 586 BCE[2] was understood as consequence of God's withdrawing from them in their resistance to Babylonian invasion. In fact, the idea that God used war to punish an apostate Israel continually reappears in the Hebrew Scriptures (Isaiah 5:26–28; Jeremiah 5:15–17; and Ezekiel 21:1–32; 23:22–28). Its corollary belief that God disciplined other nations by means of war is also widespread in the Bible (Isaiah 13; Jeremiah 46:1–10; and Nahum 2:1–9). Again, theological interpretation and explanation of a nation's fortunes in war was common in other cultures of the ancient Near East.

In Exodus 15:3 we read that "The Lord is a warrior, the Lord is his name." As a community delivered from slavery, Israel rejoiced in the defeat of its oppressors, and sang and danced in celebration of the drowning of Pharaoh's army in the Sea of Reeds (see Exodus 15). Nevertheless, to call God a warrior sounds crude to contemporary ears. The image is a particularly repugnant as an image of masculine violence. Thus, it may be prudent to suggest that the biblical image of God as warrior be viewed against its original historical context and that it not be applied today.

# Prophetic Images for God

The prophets encountered God variously: Elijah experienced God in silence (1 Kings 19:12); Isaiah, while praying in the temple in Jerusalem (Isaiah 6); Jeremiah, from before his birth (Jeremiah 1); Hosea, in his failed marriage. Amos saw God punishing Israel for failing to keep the covenant (Amos 3:1—6:14); Micah presents God as a just champion of justice whose people are to walk humbly (Micah 6:8) and in awesome visions (chapters 1 and 2). Ezekiel assured the Israelites of God's abiding presence throughout the Babylonian Exile.

## Second Isaiah

The book of Isaiah is attributed to three authors. Chapters 40 through 55 are thought to have been written by the "Second Isaiah," a Hebrew poet and theologian who lived in the time of the Babylonian Exile. He emphasizes the distance between God and humanity, yet depicts God in images drawn from human experience. The book of Second Isaiah begins with a rhetorical question: "To whom then will you liken God, or what likeness compare with him?" (Isaiah 40:18). It is not only graven images that are inadequate to describing the likeness to God; nothing and no one can be likened to God or set up as God's equal (Isaiah 40:14–25). He ends his prophecy with the conviction that God's thoughts and ways are as high above ours as heaven is above the earth. To the ancient mind, this is an almost infinite distance (cf. Isaiah 55:8–9).

Throughout, though, the prophet speaks metaphorically about God's nature and actions. The incomparable God for whom no likeness is adequate is described as a shepherd carrying lambs and leading ewes to water (Isaiah 40:11); as measuring the waters and heavens, and weighing the mountains (Isaiah 40:12); as enthroned on Earth's vaulted roof (Isaiah 40:22); as stretching the sky as if it were a curtain or a tent (Isaiah 40:22); and as the creator who gave breath to the Earth's people, who foretells what will be and who calls the pagan king Cyrus. This sublime creator is also the berserk clansman who rushes into battle, cries out like a woman in childbirth and lays waste mountains and hills, who leads the blind on their way, turning darkness into light before them. God is the maker and the helper, Israel's king and ransom payer, the one who carries Israel from birth to old age; the one and only God who makes light and darkness; whose hands founded the earth and formed the sky; the husband who acknowledges Israel once more as wife (cf. Isaiah 41:2–5; 42:5, 13–16; 44:2, 6; 45:1, 6–7; 46:3–4, 8–10; 54:4–10).

Second Isaiah states that God has no human or earthly likeness, yet the prophet uses metaphoric images for the invisible God who cannot be represented in graven image. The prophet illustrates the prime function of biblical language about God, which is to affect the imagination and evoke an active response. The biblical experience of God is not in concepts argued and reasoned, but in the Holy One who encounters us and whose reality impinges on us. Like all good metaphors, biblical God-language tweaks the imagination with intuitive certitude.

## Hosea

In the book of Hosea, God is the husband and lover of Israel (Hosea 2—3). No matter how often Israel was faithless, God remained faithful. Even when the unfaithful beloved forgets God, God still cannot leave her. In Hosea 2:14 we read:

> Therefore I will now allure her,
>     and bring her into the wilderness,
>     and speak tenderly to her.

This is a judgment against Israel; the wilderness means total privation. But God also woos Israel's heart.

> From there, I will give her her vineyards, . . .
> There she shall respond as in the days of her youth. . . .
> On that day, says the Lord, you will call me "My husband. . . ."
> (Hosea 2:15–16)

In such circumstances, where there is no other enticing voice, the heart is open to wooing, and the beloved follows her lover once more.

God says later in the book of Hosea: "How can I give you up, Ephraim? How can I hand you over, O Israel? How can I make you like Admah? How can I treat you like Zeboiim?" (Hosea 11:8). God asks if he should treat Israel like he treated the cities of Admah and Zeboium, destroyed along with Sodom and Gomorrah. God becomes anguished about Israel: "They have refused to return to me" (11:56), and "My people are bent on turning away from me" (11:7a). According to the law (cf. Deuteronomy 21:21), death was the only punishment permissible for such a stubborn child. At that point, however, God's internal struggle begins: "How shall I surrender you? Give you up?" It is the lament of a father's heart, torn between law and love. From the beginning, love has determined God's ways with his child: "When Israel was a child, I loved him. . . . I led them with cords of human kindness, with bands of love," (Hosea 11:1, 4). But Israel's answer was always to turn away. With the accusation made, punishment must be pronounced. Instead, the Father admonishes himself: "I will not execute my fierce anger; I will not again destroy Ephraim" (11:9a). The judge decides that love shall be the final word. The coexistence between God's wrath and God's love has an end, too. Hosea 11:8b is explicit: "My heart recoils within me; my compassion grows warm and tender." God undergoes the repentance that humankind refuses.

Such passion is very human, especially in the struggle between anger and love, between justice and pardon. This human feeling, together with the victory of love, is an essential part of God. "For I am God and no mortal, the Holy One in your midst, and I will not come in wrath" (Hosea 11:9b). After such self-questioning and the overthrowing of justified divine wrath in the guilty child's favor, God remains true to God's own self, in letting love be the last word.

Two metaphors for God that are not drawn from personal relationships are found in Hosea 5:12–14.

Therefore, I am like maggots to Ephraim
    and like rottenness to the house of Judah.
When Ephraim saw his sickness,
    and Judah his wound,
then Ephraim went to Assyria,
    and sent to the great king.
But he is not able to cure you
    or heal your wound.
For I will be like a lion to Ephraim,
    and like a young lion to the house of Judah.
I myself will tear and go away;
    I will carry off, and no one shall rescue.

These two images are interesting metaphors for God's dealing with infidelity: a festering sore slowly weakening the body, betrayed by its stench of rot; and a lion, pouncing upon its prey and carrying it away to rend at leisure in its lair. Their subject is God, Israel's husband and lover (Hosea 2–3). These shocking metaphors of divine activity are not Hosea's most important models for knowing and understanding God. They are, nonetheless, just as revelatory as his metaphors of God as husband, lover and mother of Israel.

# Lady Wisdom, Sophia

*Sophia* is a name used for God. *Sophia* is the Greek word for the Hebrew noun *hokmah*, "wisdom." In the Hebrew Scriptures wisdom is a woman in both the book of Proverbs and in the book of Job; her role is expanded in the books of Wisdom and Sirach.

What is the significence of Lady Wisdom? The words for *wisdom* in the three languages of the Bible's earliest editions, *hokmah* (Hebrew), *sophia* (Greek), and *sapientia* (Latin) are feminine nouns. More important, wisdom appears as a female figure in the Bible. Much is said about Lady Wisdom in a few texts. She strides into the scene as a prophetess: "Wisdom cries out in the street; in the squares she raises her voice" (Proverbs 1:20). Wisdom's origin is speculative; some scholars see it in the cult of the Egyptian goddess Maat (cf. Proverbs 8:1–21), while others maintain that Woman Wisdom is firmly rooted in the Jewish sociological and religious context. We turn to Proverbs, chapters one through nine, the principal texts where Woman Wisdom is to be found. What do they say about Lady Wisdom and her relationship with God and humanity? As the first conceived and firstborn, Wisdom's relationship with God is unique:

> The Lord created me at the beginning of his work,
>      the first of his acts of long ago.
> Ages ago I was set up,
>      at the first, before the beginning of the earth.
> When there were no depths I was brought forth,
>      when there were no springs abounding with water.
> Before the mountains had been shaped,
>      before the hills, I was brought forth. (Proverbs 8:22–25)

Wisdom is perceived as having existed with God before creation, while God is her mother. Proverbs 8 states her relation to the created world and to God:

> Then I was beside him, like a master worker;
> and I was daily his delight,
>      rejoicing before him always,
> rejoicing in his inhabited world
>      And delighting in the human race. (Proverbs 8:30–31)

Here, Wisdom is the mediator in whom God delights, and who delights in God's creation, including humanity. Her activities are equivalent to God's, and when she first appears announces:

> Then they will call upon me, but I will not answer;
> they will seek me diligently, but will not find me. (Proverbs 1:28)

Strikingly similar language can be found in the prophetic texts wherein God calls to Israel, Israel refuses response, and God reacts (e.g., Isaiah 65:2, 12; 66:4; Jeremiah 7:13, 24–27; and Hosea 2:14–15; 11:1–2).

In the opening lines of Isaiah 55, God invites the people to receive food and drink, from which they will derive life (Isaiah 53:1–3). That pursuit to be in God's presence is a recurring theme throughout the Bible. Wisdom gives life to whoever seeks and heeds her (cf. Proverbs 1:33; 3:18, 22; 4:13; 8:35; 9:6). "Whoever finds me finds life," she declares, and "all who hate me love death" (Proverbs 8:36). Wisdom also guards and keeps those who heed her (cf. Psalm 121). Also significant is the banquet she serves: "Come, eat of my bread and drink of the wine I have mixed . . . and live" (Proverbs 9:5–6). Like the God of Israel, Wisdom is a purveyor of justice: "By me kings reign, and rulers declare what is just" (Proverbs 8:15).

Other parallels between Wisdom and God reside in who she is rather than in what she does. Like God, she affects life with her very presence. In clinging to Wisdom, human beings will learn understanding, prudence and insight, which will lead to life "without dread of disaster" (Proverbs 1:33). Proverbs 3:13–18 is eloquent about life lived in Wisdom's presence:

> Happy are those who find wisdom,
>     and those who get understanding,
> for her income is better than silver,
>     and her revenue better than gold.
> She is more precious than jewels,
>     and nothing you desire can compare with her.
> Long life is in her right hand;
>     in her left hand are riches and honor.
> Her ways are ways of pleasantness,
>     and all her paths are peace.
> She is the tree of life to all those who lay hold of her;
>     those who hold her fast are called happy. (Proverbs 3:13–18)

One thing we first notice about Woman Wisdom is her power of speech. For example, in Proverbs 1:20–21 she speaks and weeps, and raises her voice and cries out (cf. Proverbs 8:1–3). She is her own authority. She is not demure and soft-spoken, rather she cajoles with promises and reproaches with threats.

Does this mean that Woman Wisdom is God? The answer is not simple. As we have seen, there are equivalents between her actions and God's, between God's presence and Wisdom's presence. What is said about Woman Wisdom is not said about any human being in the Bible.

The first nine chapters of the book of Proverbs provide images of one aspect of God's divinity in female form. Insofar as wisdom is a divine characteristic, Woman Wisdom is a personification of one aspect of God. The book of Proverbs is a door to the possibility of a female personification of God.

Such a development took place over time. The books of Wisdom and Sirach bear witness to this development. In these texts, especially the book of Wisdom, the writers refer to Woman Wisdom as simply "she." She rescued, protected, saved, guided and delivered, actions normally ascribed to God:

> She guided them along a marvelous way,
> and became a shelter to them by day,
> and a starry flame by night. (Wisdom 10:17)

The books of Sirach and Baruch identify Wisdom with the Torah. God gives the concept of Wisdom/Torah to Jacob/Israel as a way of knowledge: "She is the book of the commandments of God, the law that endures forever" (Baruch 4:1).

"In light of these narrations, descriptions and praises, reflection on Sophia's relation to the one God of Israel becomes crucial."[3] To the question of whether Woman Wisdom is God, a prudent response is that Woman Wisdom is an emanation from God, or what biblical scholar Roland Murphy calls "a communication of God." Murphy writes of Wisdom speaking "in the accents of God."[4] We must be vague because *hokmah* is not a finished concept in the Hebrew Scriptures. Thus, there are different and legitimate possibilities open to continued understanding of the concept of Woman Wisdom that are in line with the biblical tradition.

# Images for God in the Psalms

The book of Psalms, the prayer book of both Christians and Jews, contains many images for God. In it, God is often presented and prayed to as a shield (Psalm 3:3; 7:10), a judge (Psalm 7:11), my rock (18:2; 19:14; 18:31), my redeemer (Psalm 19:14), a savior (Psalm 24:5), a shepherd (Psalm 23:1, 28:9; 78:52; 80:1; 100:3), a refuge of strength (Psalm 46:1; 62:8–9), a wonder-worker (Psalm 77:14) and most worthy of praise (Psalm 47:7; 147:1; 150:1). The psalmist has hope in God (Psalm 42:6; 43:5), whom he sees as king of the earth reigning over all nations (Psalm 47:7–8), and as like no other god (Psalm 89:7). The God of the psalmist crushes the heads of his enemies (Psalm 68:21) and instructs the psalmist in his youth (Psalm 71:17), and is the one whom the psalmist thanks (Psalm 136), and with whom he is happy (Psalm 146:5).

The psalter contains three major images for God that need exploration: the Storm, the Sun and the Divine Presence.

# God and the Storm

The primary language in the psalms about God coming to the Israelites is the metaphor of the storm. Psalm 29 is explicit about God's physical manifestation, or theophany, in the storm.

> Ascribe to the Lord, O heavenly beings,
>     ascribe to the Lord glory and strength.
> Ascribe to the Lord the glory of his name;
>     worship the Lord in holy splendor.
>
> The voice of the Lord is over the waters;
>     the God of glory thunders,
>     the Lord, over mighty waters.
> The voice of the Lord is powerful;
>     the voice of the Lord is full of majesty.
>
> The voice of the Lord breaks the cedars;
>     the Lord breaks the cedars of Lebanon.
> He makes Lebanon skip like a calf,
>     and Sirion like a young wild ox.
>
> The voice of the Lord flashes forth flames of fire.
> The voice of the Lord shakes the wilderness;
>     the Lord shakes the wilderness of Kadesh.
>
> The voice of the Lord causes the oaks to whirl,
>     and strips the forest bare;
>     and in his temple all say, "Glory!"
>
> The Lord sits enthroned over the flood;
>     the Lord sits enthroned as king forever.
> May the Lord give strength to his people!
>     May the Lord bless his people with peace! (Psalm 29)

Verse one invites immortals in heaven to unite with earthly mortals in praise of the glory of God (verse 9). The second through the eighth verses describe the divine glory in the storm. Armed with thunder and lightning, God the warrior battles the chaotic waters of the void, pushing them to the edges of the cosmos to make room for creation (Genesis 1:2, 6; Psalm 104:9). Psalm 29 celebrates the warrior God's continuing victory against chaos, a conquest symbolized by the seasonal rainstorms that come off the Mediterranean Sea onto the coast of Israel. God's powers make the mountains leap and the desert writhe. The community's experience of God in the storm is reflected in the ninth verse of Psalm 29, "and in his temple all say 'Glory!'" Thus, God is exalted as king of the community, their protection: "The Lord gives strength to his people . . . the Lord blesses his people with peace" (Psalm 29:11).

The storm waters are a strong image for God; they signify both the defeat of the destructive waters of chaos and life for Israel. The rains sustained Israel's crops and provided abundant life, joyfully celebrated in the liturgy of the temple. The storm imagery in Psalm 97:1–5 is a complete description of God's life-giving power. The natural elements of clouds, darkness, fire and lightning combine with the divine qualities of righteousness and justice.

> The Lord is king! Let the earth rejoice;
> > let the many coastlands be glad!
> Clouds and thick darkness are all around him;
> > righteousness and justice are the foundation of his throne.
> Fire goes before him,
> > and consumes his adversaries on every side.
> His lightnings light up the world;
> > the earth sees and trembles.
> The mountains melt like wax before the Lord,
> > before the Lord of all the earth. (Psalm 97:1–5)

Psalm 114 describes the coming of God's power that makes earthly obstacles flee, and merges it with Israel's historical crossings of the Red Sea and of the Jordan River:

> When Israel went out from Egypt,
> > the house of Jacob from a people of strange language,
> Judah became God's sanctuary,
> > Israel his dominion.
>
> The sea looked and fled;
> > Jordan turned back.
> The mountains skipped like rams,
> > the hills like lambs.
>
> Why is it, O sea, that you flee?
> > O Jordan, that you turn back?
> O mountains, that you skip like rams?
> > O hills, like lambs?
>
> Tremble, O earth, at the presence of the Lord,
> > at the presence of the God of Jacob,
> who turns the rock into a pool of water,
> > the flint into a spring of water. (Psalm 114:1–8)

Psalms 29, 97, 114 and others (see Psalms 18, 77, 89, 98, 104; cf. Exodus 15), demonstrate the importance the experience of divine power and kingship in the storm. After a dry summer in Israel, the rains of October are especially vivid. It is surprising, then, that the autumn Feast of Tabernacles comes at the time of year when the storms begin again.

# God and the Sun

To the psalmists, the storm is only one natural image of the story of God's coming. But several psalms that speak of "seeing God" use different language to capture the immediacy of God's presence. "When shall I come and behold the face of God?" asks Psalm 42:2. Psalm 11:7 says that the "upright shall behold [God's] face," while Psalm 17:15 voices hope: "As for me, I shall behold your face in righteousness; when I awake I shall be satisfied, beholding your likeness." Psalm 27:4, 13 also voices longing:

> One thing I have asked of the Lord
>     that will I seek after;
> to live in the house of the Lord all the days of my life,
>     to behold the beauty of the Lord.
> I believe that I shall see
>     the goodness of the Lord in the land of the living.

Finally, Psalm 63:2 recounts past experience: "So I have looked upon you in the sanctuary, beholding your power and glory." These five psalms relate lived experiences of the divine as well as the hope of future experience.

What did the psalmists believe they experienced in "seeing God"? The language of seeing God's face is part of a larger complex of phrases that includes language about the light emanating from God's face. For example, the psalmists frequently request that God's face shine upon them (Psalms 31:17; 80:4–8). God's face bestows light on worshipers in Psalms 4:7 and 90:8. Worship is directed to God's face in Psalms 22:24; 24:5; 57:2 and 89:16. The language of light found in Psalm 27:1 and Psalm 43:3 seems to be part of the metaphor of God's face. One might suggest that Psalm 17:15 implies a liturgical setting: "When I awake I shall be satisfied, beholding your likeness." Perhaps, after a night of vigil, the psalmists may have expected a sunrise theophany, as suggested in the vigil psalms, 17, 27 and 63.[5]

A solar theophany can be deduced because the temple is the locus of the experience described (Psalms 27:4; 42:4; 63:3; cf. Ezekiel 8:16). Based on Ezekiel 8:16, it appears that the worshipers experienced the theophany both in the inner court and in the outer areas of the temple. This experience occurred thrice yearly when all males were commanded to make pilgrimage to Jerusalem so that "they will appear before [God]" (Exodus 23:15, 17; 34:20, 23; Deuteronomy 16:16; 31:11). Biblical commentators note that the phrase "they will appear before me" was originally "they see God." This was apparently felt to be too anthropomorphic and so was rewritten.

Witnessing a solar theophany would not have been limited to pilgrims on their way to Jerusalem, as in Psalms 42, 43 and 84, but would have included persons in the temple. The temple was "oriented," that is, facing east, and as the sun rose over the Mount of Olives, its light struck, penetrated and illuminated the temple

(Ezekiel 43:1–5). The solar theophany was brief, lasting from the sun's rise until it was above the temple.

Some psalms, such as 31 and 80, are not psalms of vigil and do not fit easily into solar theophany theory. These psalms and others, such as: 4:7; 67:2; 89:16; 90:8 and 119:135, indicate that the image of God's shining face was a broad metaphor expressing favor, concern or blessing. Perhaps it dates from an ancient solar theophany described in Deuteronomy 33:2: "The Lord came from Sinai, and dawned from Seir upon us; he shone forth from Mount Paran." In Psalm 84, the language refers specifically to the sun's rise:

> How lovely is your dwelling place,
>     O Lord of hosts!
> My soul longs, indeed it faints
>     for the courts of the Lord;
> my heart and my flesh sing for joy
>     to the living God.
>
> Even the sparrow finds a home,
>     and the swallow a nest for herself,
>     where she may lay her young,
> at your altars, O Lord of hosts,
>     my King and my God.
> Happy are those who live in your house,
>     ever singing your praise.
>
> Happy are those whose strength is in you,
>     in whose heart are the highways to Zion.
> As they go through the valley of Baca
>     they make it a place of springs;
>     the early rain also covers it with pools.
> They go from strength to strength;
>     the God of gods will be seen in Zion.
>
> O Lord God of hosts, hear my prayer;
>     give ear, O God of Jacob!
> Behold our shield, O God;
>     look on the face of your anointed.
>
> For a day in your courts is better
>     than a thousand elsewhere.
> I would rather be a doorkeeper in the house of my God
>     than live in the tents of wickedness.
> For the Lord God is a sun and shield;
>     he bestows favor and honor.
> No good thing does the Lord withhold
>     from those who walk uprightly.
> O Lord of hosts,
>     happy is everyone who trusts in you.

Like Psalm 42–43, Psalm 84 is the pilgrim's utterance of longing to experience the living God in the temple.

## Divine Presence in the Psalms

The language of seeing God is about experiencing the divine presence. The psalmists expect divine favor or blessing. The Hebrew verb *r'h*, "to see," is ambiguous; in Psalms 27:13; 42:3 and 63:3 it may mean "to experience" God. In these cases, the psalmists "saw" God, which was one way of experiencing divine power and glory. In these psalms, the experience of God is not limited to solar metaphors, but rather they use the old tradition of solar theophany or, in the cases of Psalms 17, 27 and 63, their experience of the sun to describe a single aspect of their experience of God in the temple. Ultimately, the psalmists explained their experiences using the language of solar theophany. In that respect, their experiences may be akin to the prophetic visions of Isaiah and Ezekiel.

Psalms 11:7; 17:15 and 27:4 use *hzh*, a form of the Hebrew verb *r'h* denoting prophetic vision and so used in Isaiah 6 and Ezekiel 1. Like the psalmists' experience of seeing God, the prophetic vision incorporates the language of light. Isaiah 6 describes the seraphim, the burning ones, who are angelic ministers at God's feet. Ezekiel 1:27 describes the divine presence's brilliance. What the psalmists experienced in the temple was too great to be reduced to natural phenomenon and had to draw upon solar language to express the experience of the divine.

Brilliant light was only one aspect of experience of the divine in the temple. There were other aspects, as Ezekiel describes:

> And above the dome over their heads, there was something like a throne, in appearance like sapphire; and seated above the likeness of a throne was something that seemed like a human form. Upward from what appeared like the loins I saw something like gleaming amber, something that looked like fire enclosed all around; and downward from what looked like the loins I saw something that looked like fire, and there was a splendor all around. Like the bow in a cloud on a rainy day, such was the appearance of the splendor all around. This was the appearance of the likeness of the glory of the Lord.
>
> When I saw it, I fell on my face, and I heard the voice of someone speaking. (Ezekiel 1:26 and 28)

According to 1 Kings 6:23–28, God was seated on a cherubim throne 10 cubits (15.5 feet) high. Such detail tells us that the psalmists perceived God in human terms, like a king seated on a throne. At the same time, God is seen as super human in size. Thus the psalmist reveals his hope of seeing a God who is both famliar in form but greater and more glorious than anything ever seen. The prophetic visions of Isaiah and Ezekiel, both of whom saw God, confirm this image. In the temple, internal and external perceptions merge in the experience of God that gave joy and, perhaps, even healing to those who trusted.

Using natural phenomena to evoke an experience of the divine is not unusual in the Hebrew Scriptures. As we have seen, God was also experienced in the thunderstorm, and the east wind symbolized God's destructive power. Still, the powerful image of a solar theophany requires spiritual and theological explanations. One could point to the general experience of the sun's bountiful light, its warmth and life-giving effects and ask if God's goodness (Psalm 27:13) and beauty (Psalm 27:4) are experienced the same way. The sun could have served as symbol not only of God's immanence but also of divine transcendence. Biblical tradition records the notion that "no one shall see me and live," which corresponds with the fact that one cannot directly look into the sun (Exodus 33:20 and 23). Thus, Moses could not see God's face (Exodus 33 and 34); neither could the Israelites who had hoped to see God's face (Psalms 17:15 and 42:3). They could not see the depths of the divine.

Sometimes natural images of storm or sun or wind sufficed to express the experience of God's glory in the temple. Consequently, some biblical passages combine images of natural phenomena for completeness. Ezekiel 43:1–5, which describes the procession of God's *kabod*, "glory," combines solar language with storm imagery:

> Then he brought me to the gate, the gate facing east. And there, the glory of the God of Israel was coming from the east; the sound was like the sound of mighty waters; and the earth shone with his glory. The vision I saw was like the vision that I had seen when he came to destroy the city, and like the vision that I had seen by the river Chebar; and I fell upon my face. As the glory of the Lord entered the temple by the gate facing east, the spirit lifted me up and brought me into the inner court; and the glory of the Lord filled the temple.

The divine glory is deafening, "like the sound of mighty waters." The glory seems to proceed like the procession of the sun. The combined solar and storm language in Ezekiel 43:1–5 raises the important matter that such hybrid imagery suggests the omnipresent nature of God, so great that one could not easily picture it with a single natural image; thus God is truly supernatural. Psalm 50:1–3 also combines imagery from different realms of nature:

> The mighty one, God the Lord,
>      speaks and summons the earth
>      from the rising of the sun to its setting.
> Out of Zion, the perfection of beauty,
>      God shines forth.
> Our God comes and does not keep silence,
>      before him is a devouring fire,
>      and a mighty tempest all around him.

The first and second verses apply solar language to God, while the third verse uses the image of a devouring fire for the divine procession. This tension illustrates the paradox of experiencing the divine glory. On the one hand, the Israelites understood that God's glory could be experienced by way of natural phenomena and expressed in the language of storm and sun. It could be identified as dwelling in the temple, and its power could be gauged and felt by its believers. The prophet Ezekiel describes glory's departure from the temple (Ezekiel 10) and envisions its return (Ezekiel 43). Similarly, the glory of God accompanied the Israelites in their 40-year wilderness trek. On the other hand, there were limits to human experience of divine glory. Though its external manifestations are observable, its depths are too brilliant to be plumbed and apprehended by the mortal mind. Exodus 33 and 34 note that even Moses, the great leader chosen by God, had only a partial experience of the divine. Nevertheless, for the psalmists such an experience often culminated a pilgrimage to Jerusalem and the temple. Following the experience of "seeing God," one psalmist exults in joy and confidence:

> So I have looked upon you in the sanctuary,
>     beholding your power and glory.
> Because your steadfast love is better than life
>     my lips will praise you.
> So I will bless you as long as I live;
>     I will lift up my hands and call on your name.
>
> My soul is satisfied as with a rich feast,
>     and my mouth praises you with joyful lips
> when I think of you on my bed,
>     and meditate on you in the watches of the night;
> for you have been my help,
>     and in the shadow of your wings I sing for joy.
> My soul clings to you;
>     your right hand upholds me.
>
> But those who seek to destroy my life
>     shall go down into the depths of the earth;
> they shall be given over to the power of the sword,
>     they shall be prey for jackals.
> But the king shall rejoice in God;
>     all who swear by him shall exult,
>     for the mouths of liars will be stopped. (Psalm 63:2–11)

These are the words of a person at peace, thanks to God. This does not mean that all of life's troubles have disappeared, as verses nine and ten show, but rather that this person has found peace with God, the true reality. All other difficulties will resolve themselves in due course. This is the experience of God, who comes to save and be with those who believe.

# Feminine Images for God

The Hebrew Scriptures use feminine images to speak of God. For example, in the book of Isaiah, God is a mother: "Can a woman forget her nursing child, or show no compassion for the child of her womb? Even these may forget, yet I will not forget you" (Isaiah 49:15).

Any woman who has been pregnant knows well her preoccupation with her unborn child. To forget would be unthinkable; so it is with God's relationship with each of us. Each one is special and no one is ever forgotten.

Moreover, God is the mother who conceives, bears and gives birth to Israel (Numbers 11:12 and Deuteronomy 32:18), and a midwife (Psalm 22:9–10; and Isaiah 66:6–9). In Isaiah 66:10–14, God is the nursing mother who cuddles her child and wipes away its tears. Furthermore, God is the sheltering mother in Psalms 17:1–2, 6–7, 8–10; 57:2, 8–9, 10–12; 61:2–3, 4–5, 6, 9; 91:1–2, 3–4; and 14:16, while in Nehemiah 9:13–21, Isaiah 25:6–10 and Wisdom 16:20–21 God provides food, water and clothing, traditionally women's work.

## God Is Faithful in Caring for Us

The prophets assured believers that God never forsook them and constantly accompanied them. Isaiah says:

> Now thus says the Lord,
>     he who created you, O Jacob,
>     he who formed you, O Israel:
> Do not fear, for I have redeemed you;
>     I have called you by name, you are mine.
> When you pass through the waters, I will be with you;
>     and through the rivers, they shall not overwhelm you;
> when you walk through fire you shall not be burned,
>     and the flame shall not consume you. (Isaiah 43:1–2)

The prophet Hosea spoke of God's wish for a mutual and loving relationship with us. When the people of the Northern Kingdom (often referred to as "Ephraim" in the Hebrew Scriptures) were turning to other gods, God yearned nostalgically for when their relationship was as tender as that between loving parent and child:

> Yet it was I who taught Ephraim to walk,
>     I took them up in my arms;
>     but they did not know that I healed them.
> I led them with cords of human kindness,
>     with bonds of love.
> I was to them like those
>     who lift infants to their cheeks.
>     I bent down to them and fed them. (Hosea 11:3–4)

Jeremiah beautifully expresses God's fidelity: "I have loved you with an everlasting love; therefore I have continued my faithfulness to you" (Jeremiah 31:3).

The psalmist clearly notes that forgiveness accompanies fidelity: "God does not deal with us according to our sins" (Psalm 103:10), and "The Lord is gracious and merciful, slow to anger, and abounding in steadfast love" (Psalm 145:8).

A story from the Jewish tradition best illustrates the point: A devout rabbinical student asked his rabbi: "Master, how is it that the closer I come to God the farther away God seems to get?"

Smiling, the rabbi replied: "My student, have you ever seen a parent teach a child to walk? First, the parent stands very close to the child and beckons it to take a few steps. Then, the parent moves away from the child. Each time the child walks back to the parent, the parent retreats farther still, and so increasing the distance between them in order that the child will learn to walk. So it is with God, a truly loving parent."

# For Discussion

1. Is it shocking to use animal imagery to think of God?

2. How do you react to the Bible's feminine and maternal images for God?

3. Have you ever experienced God as your Redeemer or as manifested in storms or in the sun?

4. What is your favorite image for God from the Hebrew Scriptures? Why?

# Jesus the Icon of God and His Images for God

Whoever has seen me has seen the Father.

(John 14:9)

The Greek word *icon*, "image" in English, encompasses all types of images, not just the flat, two-dimensional paintings rendered on wood, but also sculptures, and even some human beings. Icons of God, of Jesus Christ, of Mary and of the saints abound in the Eastern Church.

# Chapter Four

The New Testament church understood Jesus to be the icon *par excellence* of God, the human being in whom God is to be encountered. As the scriptures point out, who sees Jesus sees God the Father. Jesus is the image of the invisible God.

What is original about the Christian understanding of God is its identification of God with Jesus of Nazareth. The revelation of God in Jesus Christ is not solely in the prophetic words he uttered, as was the case with the Hebrew prophets. Rather Christ's person communicates God. There is an identification between God and Christ. The prologue of the gospel according to John makes this clear:

> In the beginning was the Word, and the Word was with God, and the Word was God. . . . And the Word became flesh and lived among us, and we have seen his glory, the glory as of a Father's only son, full of grace and truth. (John 1:1, 14)

There is a kind of parallel prologue in the Letter to the Hebrews:

> Long ago God spoke to our ancestors in many and various ways by the prophets, but in these last days, he has spoken to us by a Son, whom he appointed heir of all things, through whom he also created the worlds. He is the reflection of God's glory and the exact imprint of God's very being, and he sustains all things by his powerful word. (Hebrews 1:1–3)

For the writers of the New Testament, God is manifest in the person of Jesus Christ. Nevertheless, the New Testament reserves the Greek title *ho theos*, "God," to the Father of Jesus Christ. Jesus is the Son of God. This title, of all applied to him, is the most important.

# Jesus the Son of God

In the infancy narrative in the Gospel of Luke, one succinct statement summarizes the gospel's belief in who Jesus is: "The Holy Spirit will come upon you, and the power of the Most High will overshadow you; therefore the child to be born will be holy; he will be called Son of God" (Luke 1:35).

The Hebrew Scriptures applied the title *Son of God* both to the people of Israel and to their kings. In those contexts, the title did not imply divinity but indicated that God's adoption of the Israelites and of their king bound them in a relationship as intimate as that between parent and child.

In the Christian Scriptures the title *Son of God*, as applied to Jesus Christ, is a post-Resurrection interpretation by the early church. Mark's gospel reinterprets the title to fit that gospel's primary focus, suffering. The high point of the Gospel of Mark is the centurion's recognition of the crucified Jesus as the Son of God (Mark 15:39). Mark identifies Jesus as the Son of God and defines the title as the Suffering Servant (cf. Isaiah 42:1–4; 49:1–6; 50:4–9; 52:13–53:12).

Is Jesus God? When people ask, they presume that we know who God is. The question means: Can you fit Jesus Christ into your God-picture? We know quite a lot about Jesus. Yet, do we know enough about God to answer the question? The best Christian answer has always been: We do not exactly know who is God, but do know that by looking at Jesus we can discover who is God. The heart of Christian faith is *not* that Jesus is part of God, or resembles God, but rather that the one whom we speak of as God was and is present and discoverable in Jesus of Nazareth.

An idea of such magnitude is difficult to grasp. For many people, the word *God* denotes a remote being defined in dry dogma, who keeps a detached and dignified distance from humanity's rough-and-tumble life. If one means *that* God when they ask: "Is Jesus God?" the answer would have to be no. It would always be nonsense to imagine that Jesus is identified with that God. Why should we believe in such a God?

Instead, suppose we begin with the God Jesus knew, the passionate and compassionate God in the Hebrew Scriptures. What might that God be like? That God is great enough to be creator of the world and tender enough to care for young birds when they call. That God hears the cry of Israel when they are in slavery. Of that God, the prophet Isaiah says, "The Lord has bared his holy arm" (Isaiah 52:10), which, in plain English means that God has rolled up his sleeves to work with us.

If you begin with this understanding of God and ask "What might this God look like as a human?" then the life and death of Jesus of Nazareth show the true God as a human being, God incarnate, in traditional Christian language.

This is a God with a human face, that of Jesus of Nazareth, who is clearly recognizable as God when he dies on the cross, bearing the weight of the world's evil and pain. Moreover, this is a God who became human without permitting violence to destroy the essential divine nature. This is the God of true and sovereign love; such a God cannot remain detached and impersonal. The true God wears a human face crowned with thorns.

Throughout his life, Jesus Christ was not concerned with abstract teachings about God. Jesus was a Jewish man aflame with God's love, and he practiced it whenever people were in need. Jesus' love was vital, personal and immediate. The closer we are to the original Jesus—the storyteller, the healer, the one who welcomes outcasts and who delcares God's judgment upon those who reject the way of peace and justice—the closer we are to recognizing the face of the living God. Christianity centers on a young Jew telling stories about the kingdom of God, healing the sick, confronting the powerful, and eventually dying and rising in defeat of death. "That," Christianity says, "is what it means to be God."

Thus, when we ask, is Jesus God? it is best to turn the question around: "Is it true that the living God was uniquely and personally present in Jesus?" This answer cannot remain abstract doctrine. If we reply, "Yes," we commit ourselves to a journey of exploration into God by learning of the life, teachings, death and resurrection of Jesus. The journey cannot be private or self-centered. If we begin by recognizing the rich, forgiving, healing love of the true God as found in the face of Jesus Christ, we must join in God's work of bringing healing and love to the world.

When we explore the question of Jesus and God, we uncover another question: "What would it look like if people today were captivated by the Spirit of Jesus?" At its best, the church consists of people struggling daily to answer this question in their lives, not just with words but with action and stories and symbols. That is how the historical Jesus who lived 2,000 years ago is alive and active in the history being made today.

In short, we believe that God became one of us in the person of Jesus. In the resurrection of Jesus, something momentous happened. God broke the bonds of death. Since then, nothing has been the same. God is now Emmanuel, God with us.

# Jesus the Wisdom of God

Another New Testament image relates Jesus to the wisdom of God. In the Wisdom literature of the Hebrew Scriptures, Wisdom is a woman. Consistent with this personification, *wisdom* is a female noun in Hebrew, *hokmah,* and in Greek, *sophia.* The opening chapter of the book of Proverbs shows Woman Wisdom speaking publicly, as the prophets do. (Proverbs 1:20–33) In Proverbs 8:1—9:6, she speaks of herself as source of insight, truth and strength, and as one who participated in God's work of participant creation.

Throughout Sirach 24, Woman Wisdom speaks of her presence everywhere. She dwells among the people, in the tabernacle of the wilderness, until she goes to dwell in Jerusalem: "Then the Creator of all things gave me a command, and my Creator chose the place of my tent" (Sirach 24:8). Woman Wisdom is identical to the divine presence.

The book of Wisdom, written close to the time of Jesus, describes more fully the qualities of Woman Wisdom. She is "the fashioner of all things" (Wisdom 7:22) and the mother of all good things (Wisdom 7:11–12). She is presented as having all the attributes of God. As Marcus Borg states: "Sophia is closely associated with God, at times becoming indistinguishable from God in terms of the functions and qualities ascribed to her, so that one may speak of a 'functional equivalency' between Sophia and God."[1]

In the New Testament, there are many passages associating Jesus and Wisdom. The gospels quote Jesus as saying, "Therefore also the Wisdom of God said, 'I will send them prophets and apostles, some of whom they will kill and persecute, so that this generation may be charged with the blood of all the prophets shed since the foundation of the world'" (Luke 11:49–50; see also Matthew 23:34–45). What seems most important in this quotation is the introductory phrase, where Jesus speaks of divine Wisdom. Speaking her words, Jesus is the emissary of Wisdom. Theologian Elizabeth A. Johnson comments: "Sophia is present in and with her envoy, Jesus, pervading and embracing, containing and sustaining, indeed personally grounding him."[2] In another passage from the Gospel of Luke, Jesus speaks of himself as a child of Wisdom (Luke 7:33–35).

To the apostle Paul, Wisdom is central to describing Jesus. He speaks explicitly of him as the Wisdom of God in the First Letter to the Corinthians: "But we proclaim Christ crucified, a stumbling block to Jews and foolishness to Gentiles, but to those who are the called, both Jews and Greeks, Christ the power of God and the wisdom of God" (1 Corinthians 1:23–24).

A few lines later, Paul proclaims, "[God] is the source of your life in Christ Jesus, who became for us wisdom from God" (1 Corinthians 1:30a). It seems that Paul understood Jesus to be both the Wisdom of God and the wisdom from God. Commenting on this Pauline text, Johnson concludes:

> Using the female figure of personified Wisdom . . . to speak of Jesus the Christ offers an augmented field of metaphors with which to interpret his saving significance and rootedness in God in ways that relieve the monopoly of male images of Logos and Son. . . . This leads to the realization that as Sophia, incarnate Jesus, even in his human maleness, can be thought to be revelatory of the graciousness of God imaged as female.[3]

There is further connection between Jewish language about Wisdom and Paul's language about Jesus. Paul speaks of Christ as existing with God from eternity, and as taking part in creation (cf. 1 Corinthians 8:6). Upon this last matter, Paul expands:

> [Christ] is the image of the invisible God, the firstborn of all creation; for in him all things in heaven and on earth were created things visible and invisible, whether thrones or dominions or rulers or powers—all things have been created through him and for him. He himself is before all things, and in him all things hold together. (Colossians 1:15–17)

This echoes the descriptions of Wisdom in the books of Proverbs and Wisdom. Paul was shaped by the Jewish Wisdom/Sophia tradition. He seems not only to describe Jesus in the language of divine Wisdom but also to identify him with Wisdom. For Paul and his readers, Jesus is the embodiment of the Wisdom of God.

# Images for God Presented by Jesus

One way of understanding Jesus is as God's storyteller. We all love a good story, especially one told by a skillfull storyteller. I remember my grandfather telling us stories about the "old country," and I still remember how lively he became—twinkling eyes and emotion-filled voice—as he told these tales.

When I was in grade school, my third-grade teacher told us stories from the Bible and about the saints, capturing my imagination forever. Years later, in college, a favorite professor continued that tradition, captivating our class every week as he began his lecture with a story. Later in life, some of my rabbi friends exchanged stories with me that continually kindled my imagination.

Stories were powerful tools for a teacher. Jesus was a master storyteller. The gospels are full of the stories he told. One could almost begin a gospel with the line, "Once upon a time, in a far-off country, there lived a great storyteller." The stories that Jesus told are called parables. These stories often reveal something about the nature of God.[4]

## God the Gracious Employer

In the Gospel of Matthew is a story usually referred to as the parable of the laborers of the vineyard. It may be more aptly called the parable of God the gracious employer:

> For the kingdom of heaven is like a landowner who went out early in the morning to hire laborers for his vineyard. After agreeing with the laborers for the usual daily wage, he sent them into his vineyard. When he went out about nine o'clock, he saw others standing idle in the marketplace; and he said to them, "You also go into the vineyard, and I will pay you whatever is right." So they went. When he went out again about noon and about three o'clock, he did the same. And about five o'clock he went out and found others standing around; and he said to them, "Why are you standing here idle all day?" They said to him, "Because no one has hired us." He said to them, "You also go into the vineyard." When evening came, the owner of the vineyard said to his manager, "Call the laborers and give them their pay, beginning with the last and then going to the first." When those hired about five o'clock came; each of them received the usual daily wage. Now when the first came, they thought they would receive more; but each of them also received the usual daily wage. And when they received it, they grumbled against the landowner, saying, "These last worked only one hour, and you have made them equal to us who have borne the burden of the day and the scorching heat." But he replied to one of them, "Friend, I am doing you no wrong; did you not agree with me for the usual daily wage?" Take what belongs to you and go; I choose to give to this last the same as I give to you. Am I not allowed to do what I choose with what belongs to me? Or are you envious because I am generous?" So the last will be first, and the first will be last. (Matthew 20:1–16)

The parable takes place in the familiar world of Jesus' time, where day laborers are hired at sunup and are paid at sundown, in accordance with Jewish practice as outlined in the Torah (Leviticus 19:13; Deuteronomy 24:14–15). A *denarius* was a normal day's pay for a manual laborer hired by the day, but insufficient for supporting a family at the subsistence level.

Gradually, though, the unusual details in the story shift the parable subtly to a deeper level of meaning. Instead of sending his manager, the landowner, who represents God, goes himself to the marketplace to hire laborers (verse 8). Throughout the day, he hires workers, even at the eleventh hour (5:00 PM). The reason those standing idle were not hired during his earlier recruitment visits is left unexplained. The first group of workers is hired with an oral contract for the normal day's wage. Although the first group has a contract and the second group of laborers has only their trust in the master's sense of justice, both groups, in reality, depend on the landowner's trustworthiness. In the climax, when every worker is paid the same wage, the second group of laborers is ignored in order to focus on the first and the last groups.

The final scene contains the disturbing element that makes the tale a parable, rather than the illustration of logical point. On the landowner's order, those hired last are the first paid and receive a full day's pay. Those hired first, then expect to receive more money (verse 10) but receive only the agreed-upon wage. Matthew's readers share the concern of the workers who worked the longest. They, too, assume the same standard of justice, equal pay for equal work.

The parable disturbs because it challenges and reverses conventional values, such as the sense of justice and fairness of Matthew's readers. This is one reason why Matthew chose to preserve and insert it here. Matthew understands the parable allegorically, so that the landowner is the eschatological judge, either God or Jesus, who is indeed "good," and the payment of wages at day's end is the last judgment. In Matthew's view, the words "first" and "last" refer to "insiders"—Christians who have worked long and faithfully—and to the latecomers, the "outsiders" who have not.

This parable deals with resentment toward others who have received the grace of God we usually affirm only in theory. It is instructive to compare verses 10 and 12. Those who worked all day begin not by objecting to the grace others received but by expecting to receive more than the others. When they receive their day's pay, the just fulfillment of the contract to which they agreed, they object not to the sum paid them but to the fact that the partial-day workers were made their equals. The first receive what they have by justice; the last receive what they have— equality—by grace. This the first find unbearable, and it is their objection to the landowner's (God's) gracious acceptance of others as equals that alienates them. In view of this, the landowner addresses the complainer from the first group with the distancing word *friend* (verse 13).

About this, John R. Donahue comments: "This God loves the person who is faithful throughout the day, as well as the one called at the last hour."[5] The parable invites reflection upon the sovereignty of the good God with whom we cannot bargain. Likewise, while affirming the sovereign grace of God, it rejects presuming grace. Grace is always God's to bestow.

# The Parables of Luke, Chapter 15

In the fifteenth chapter of the Gospel of Luke there are three parables that require the reader to reflect on the nature of God. All three are about loss: the parable of the lost sheep (Luke 15:3–7), the parable of the lost coin (Luke 15:8–10) and the parable of the lost son (Luke 15:11–32).

# The Parable of the Lost Sheep

> Now all the tax collectors and sinners were coming near to listen to him. And the Pharisees and the scribes were grumbling and saying, "This fellow welcomes sinners and eats with them."
>
> So he told them this parable: "Which one of you, having a hundred sheep and losing one of them, does not leave the ninety-nine in the wilderness and go after the one that is lost until he finds it? When he has found it, he lays it on his shoulders and rejoices. And when he comes home, he calls together his friends and neighbors, saying to them, 'Rejoice with me, for I have found my sheep that was lost.' Just so, I tell you, there will be more joy in heaven over one sinner who repents than over ninety-nine righteous persons who need no repentance." (Luke 15:1–7)

In its first and second verses, chapter 15 presents a new setting. In the previous chapter, Jesus was invited to eat a Sabbath meal with the leader of the Pharisees (Luke 14:1), and the sayings that followed grew from that incident. Now the Pharisees and the Scribes "murmur" or "grumble" because Jesus eats with tax collectors and sinners. The Greek verb *to murmur* is also used to describe the Israelites' murmuring against Moses. It had been used earlier in this gospel, foreshadowing the murmuring against Jesus.

It is important to understand the role of the tax collectors and why Jesus' table fellowship with such outcasts is shocking to the Pharisees. They would have classed as sinners not only those people who broke moral laws but also those who did not observe and maintain the ritual purity practiced by the Pharisees. In their worldview, tax collectors were examples of those who broke ritual purity by handling money.

To the Pharisees, the scandal was that Jesus played host and broke bread with such outcasts. The same God who showed mercy to the apostate Israelites in the wilderness rejoices over the salvation of every lost person, like a shepherd who rejoices in recovering his lost sheep, or the woman who rejoices in finding her lost coin. The question this story poses to us is whether we join in the celebration. But to celebrate with God one must also share in God's mercy.

In the first story (Luke 15:3–7), the shepherd leaves his 99 sheep to search for the lost one. This parable reflects economic life in biblical Palestine, principally agriculture and the tending of livestock; metaphorically, it refers to God as Israel's shepherd in the Hebrew Scriptures.

> He will feed his flock like a shepherd;
>> he will gather the lambs in his arms,
>> and carry them in his bosom,
> and gently lead the mother sheep. (Isaiah 40:11)

This image of God as shepherd appears frequently in the Psalms (e.g., 23:1–4; 28:9; 78:52; 80:1; 100:3) and in the writings of the prophets (Jeremiah 31:10; Ezekiel

34:11–22; Zechariah 13:7). In the New Testament, the image is found only in Jesus' parables. Both in the Hebrew Scriptures and in the Christian literature, the shepherd served as image for religious leaders who, at times, like hirelings, did not serve their flocks well. The irony of the parable is that a human shepherd would never risk an entire flock of sheep to search for a lost lamb. Nevertheless, the divine shepherd is as concerned with a single lost sheep as he is for the entire flock.

This positive shepherd image offered both in the Hebrew Scriptures and the New Testament is in sharp contrast with historical reality. By the first century, shepherds had acquired a reputation as shiftless, thieving, trespassing hirelings. Rabbis listed shepherding—along with camel driving, sailoring, gambling with dice, cloth dyeing and tax collection—as a despised trade. The Pharisees espoused this estimation of shepherds. Their low regard for shepherds is an important context for understanding this parable. Jesus answers their criticism of his acceptance of such sinners with a parable casting God as a shepherd.

The parable's conclusion reflects its Lucan setting. The calling together of friends and neighbors to celebrate better fits the parable of the woman who found her lost coin than it does the parable about the faithful shepherd (verse 9).

Jesus' comment to the Pharisees and Scribes about the parable's meaning is important. The joy, God's celebration at the repentance of a sinner, connects the conclusion of the parable to the second verse's reference to Jesus' eating with "sinners." By implication, Jesus' breaking bread with sinners reflects God's gracious spirit toward those held in contempt.

The contrast with the 99 righteous persons creates a tension requiring a reversal of the self-righteous Pharisees' and Scribes' estimation of tax collectors and other sinners. On the one hand, the self-righteous are the 99 safe sheep, while on the other hand, God delights more in the return of the sinners, the lost sheep. The parable is doubly scandalous because it reminds the smug Pharisees and Scribes how removed they are from God. The celebration of the coming of the kingdom was taking place in Jesus' table fellowship with the outcasts, but the Pharisees and Scribes were missing it.

## The Parable of the Lost Coin

What woman having ten silver coins, if she loses one, does not light a lamp, sweep the house and search carefully until she finds it? When she has found it, she calls together her friends and neighbors, saying, "Rejoice with me, for I have found the coin that I had lost." Just so, I tell you, there is joy in the presence of the angels of God over one sinner who repents (Luke 15:8–10).

The parable of the lost coin is found only in the Gospel of Luke and is twin to that of the lost sheep. This time, God is a poor woman with ten coins. Scholar John R. Donohue points out that:

To compare God to a woman would shock and surprise the audience and challenge their fundamental image of God. The hearers are now challenged to see the searching woman as metaphor for God's searching love that paves the way for new ways of thinking about how God acts toward the sinner and the outcast. God seeks them out and rejoices more over finding them than over the presence of the righteous. The inclusion of the woman as the protagonist here also reflects Luke's interest in the gifts and roles of women in the community.[6]

A *drachma* was the Greek silver coin equivalent to the Roman *denarius*, a day's wage, not a great sum. Otherwise, the parable's point would be lost if the coin were of great value. After all, who would not search for a lost fortune? Nevertheless, the parable points to the human reaction of prizing more what is lost, even if its value were less than what one possesses. The woman, with a small dowry or few savings, will search tirelessly before accepting the loss of a single coin. Typical of her time, her house is windowless with only a dirt floor and a small door. Three actions characterize her urgent response to losing a coin: She lights a lamp, sweeps the house and searches carefully. On finding it, she rejoices and calls her friends (the word is the female plural in Greek) to celebrate.

In this parable, the difference in the relative value of the lost coin and that of the remaining nine is not noted (verse 10), unlike the way the value of one sheep is compared with the value of the remaining flock of 99 (verse 7). This parable focuses sharply on God's joy in recovering what had been lost, while the question of the righteous needing no repentance is no longer a concern. In this context, repentance is not the point, rather it is God's joy over those who respond to divine mercy.

## Reflections on the Lost Sheep and the Lost Coins

In both parables, rejoicing calls for celebration, which may be exaggerated for emphasis. The points of the parables are not to call sinners to repent but to call the righteous to join in the celebration. Whether or not one joins in the celebration is all-important because it reveals whether one's relationships are based on merit or on mercy. Those who find God's mercy offensive exclude themselves from divine grace and so cannot celebrate with the angels when a sinner repents.

These parables retain the power to expose the roots of bitterness in us whenever we feel that God is too good to others and not good enough to us. Typically, we want mercy for ourselves and justice for others, but the Lucan parables call for our celebration of God's mercifulness not only toward us but also toward those excluded from our fellowship.

An example of this is the Jewish story of the good fortune of a hard-working farmer. The Lord appeared to a farmer and offered him three wishes. The Lord's sole condition was that the farmer's neighbor would receive double of whatever he had wished. Scarcely believing his good fortune, the farmer first wished for 100 cattle. He was immediately overjoyed at receiving the 100 cattle, until he saw that his neighbor received 200. Next, the farmer wished for 100 acres of land and again was filled with joy, until he saw that his neighbor received 200 acres of land. Rather than celebrate God's goodness, the farmer could not escape feeling envious and slighted because his neighbor had received more than he had. Finally, he stated his third wish: that God strike him blind in one eye. At this, God wept.

The parables of the lost sheep and the lost coin expose the grudging spirit that often prevents us from receiving God's mercy. Only those who can celebrate God's grace towards others can experience that mercy themselves.

## The Prodigal Son, the Waiting Father and the Elder Brother

There was a man who had two sons. The younger said to his father, "Father, give me the share of the property that will belong to me." So he divided his property between them. A few days later the younger son gathered all he had and traveled to a distant country, and there he squandered his property in dissolute living. When he had spent everything, a severe famine took place throughout that country, and he began to be in need. So he went and hired himself out to one of the citizens of that country, who sent him to his fields to feed the pigs. He would gladly have filled himself with the pods that the pigs were eating; and no one gave him anything. But when he came to himself he said, "How many of my father's hired hands have bread enough and to spare, but here I am dying of hunger! I will get up and go to my father, and I will say to him, 'Father, I have sinned against heaven and before you; I am no longer worthy to be called your son; treat me like one of your hired hands.'" So he set off and went to his father. But while he was far off, his father saw him and was filled with compassion; he ran and put his arms around him and kissed him. Then the son said to him, "Father, I have sinned against heaven and before you; I am no longer worthy to be called your son." But the father said to his slaves, "Quickly, bring out a robe—the best one—and put it on him; put a ring on his finger and sandals on his feet. And get the fatted calf and kill it, and let us eat and celebrate; for this son of mine was dead and is alive again; he was lost and is found!" And they began to celebrate.

Now his elder son was in the field, and when he came and approached the house, he heard music and dancing. He called one of the slaves and asked what was going on. He replied, "Your brother has come, and your father has killed the fatted calf, because he has him back safe." Then he became angry and refused to go in. His father came out and began to plead with him. But he answered his father, "Listen! For all these years, I have been working like a slave for you, and I have never disobeyed your command; yet, you have never given me even a young goat so that I might celebrate with my friends. But when this son of yours came back, who has devoured your property with prostitutes, you killed the fatted calf for him!" Then the father said to him, "Son, you are always with me, and all that is mine is yours. But we had to celebrate and rejoice, because this brother of yours was dead and has come to life; he was lost and has been found." (Luke 15:11–32)

The title one gives to this parable, found only in the Gospel of Luke, divulges one's understanding of its theme and structure. To call it "The Prodigal Son" merely emphasizes its first half, while neglecting its second half. To call it "A Man Had Two Sons" focuses on the father's relationship with his sons, and recognizes that this is a two-peaked tale. To call it "The Compassionate Father and the Angry Brother" compares two ways of receiving the lost person. The virtue of the title "The Prodigal Son, the Waiting Father and the Elder Brother" is its recognition of each character's significance, thereby calling the reader's attention to the shifts in narrative point of view from the younger son to the father to the elder son. Alternatively, the parable may be looked at as having two parts: the father's response to the younger son (verses 12–24) and his response to the elder son (verses 25–32).

If chapter 15 is the center of the Gospel of Luke, as most scholars maintain, then "The Prodigal Son, the Waiting Father and the Elder Brother" is the paragon of parables. Drawn from family life, with which most everyone can identify, the parable contrasts the responses of the two men to the return of a prodigal.

Verse 11, the parable's opening line, identifies the story's three characters. Significantly, Jesus does not begin this parable with the conjunction "or" used to introduce the parable of the lost coin. This parable is not just a third version of the first two contained in this chapter of Luke's gospel. It complements and extends them with its theme of restoration (verses 24, 32). Whereas Jesus stated this theme as interpretation of the first two parables, in this third parable the father, who represents God, voices it. Moreover, the first two parables merely allude to celebrating, while in this parable the celebration in fact occurs, with the elder son's reaction to the celebration being the vital dramatic element of the story's second part.

The introduction identifies the siblings as sons and not as brothers, focusing on their filial relationship with their father but leaving their fraternal relationship to be dealt with later. The difficulties in the relationship between sons and father are deeply rooted in ancient Israelite tradition as in the examples of Cain and Abel, Ishmael and Isaac, Jacob and Esau, and Joseph and his brothers. Because the Israelites were descendants of Jacob, a younger brother, the younger son is favored in the stories of Israel's ancestral heritage. The great question in this parable is how would Jesus treat the conflict between younger and elder brothers?

Jesus does not introduce this parable with his usual question: "And which man [or father] among you . . . ?" (cf. 11:5, 11; 14:5, 28; 15:4). If such were the case, the audience would immediately identify with the younger son. To avoid his audience's missing the story's point, Jesus closes off identification with the father from the outset.

Another remarkable feature of this parable is the preponderance of dialogue over narration. The first part contains three speeches by the prodigal younger son: his request, an interior monologue and his confession. In both parts, the father's words are the climax of the parable. Two conversations propel the second part: the first, between the elder son and the slave, and the second, between the elder son and his father. The parable can be outlined thus:

I. Part One (15:11–24)

    A. Request of the younger son (verse 12b)

    B. Interior monologue of the younger son (verses 17b–19)

    C. Confession of the younger son (verse 21b)

    D. Directive of the father (verses 22b–24)

II. Part Two (15:25–32)

    A. Slave's explanation (verse 27b)

    B. Elder son's outburst to his father (verses 29b–30)

    C. Father's explanation to his elder son (verses 31b–32)

Considering this structure, let us analyze this parable.

## Analysis of Part One (Luke 15:11–24)

The younger son asks his father to grant him the share of the family estate that he is to inherit at the father's death. Such an early granting of patrimonial inheritance to a son might occur in case of the son's marriage, but no such rationale is given. The laws regarding inheritance were clear: an estate may only be divided after the owners death. The younger son's demand was personally disrespectful of his father and legally irregular. He was breaking the family ties and treating his father as though he were already dead. Appropriately, Jesus reports the father's response: "So, he divided his life [*bios*] between them," reads the Greek. Once granted his request, the younger son forfeits any further claims upon his father's estate, as he acknowledges in verse 19.

    The son converts his share of the patrimony to cash, but the father retains control of the rest of the estate according to Mosaic law, which may have been designed to protect the rights of an eldest son against usurpation by a favorite younger son. The elder would later receive a double portion of the inheritance (cf. Deuteronomy 21:17).

    The younger son's actions track his progressive estrangement from his family. He moved to a distant Gentile country where he dissipated his patrimony in fast living, falling first into poverty and then privation. Once at the bottom, he is forced to work tending the swine, an abomination to Jesus' Jewish audience (cf. Leviticus 11:7 and Deuteronomy 14:8). So pronounced was the prodigal's fall, and so desperate was his need that he desired to eat his fill of the pods he fed the swine. He had harvested the bitter fruit of foolishness. His destitution was complete.

    The return of the prodigal son begins in the mire of the swine pen. There, he "came to himself" (Luke 15:17), a phrase pregnant with implication, leaving much to the reader's imagination. After an insightful self-reckoning, the prodigal decides to reclaim his identity by first admitting to himself that he is undeserving to be called his father's son. He resolves to leave the far country and return to his land and father, as long before Jacob had responded to God's call to "return to your country and to your kindred" in Genesis 32:9. The expression "he came to himself" (Luke

15:17) affirms the human capacity to renounce foolish error and reclaim one's heritage and potential. The son realized that he no longer held any legal claim on his father's goods and that he no longer had the moral right to be addressed as "son." But if not as a son, perhaps his father would readmit him to the household as a slave, a life better than that which relegated him to tending swine.

Verses 17–19 are the prodigal's interior monologue and the speech he prepared for his father. That the son has "come to himself" (15:17) controls all that follows. He is not just seeking to improve his circumstances; he realizes that he has sinned against both God and his father. The speech for his father is in four parts: an address, "Father," (verse 18); a confession, "I have sinned"; an admission of contrition, "I am no longer worthy"; and a petition, "Treat me like one of your hired hands" (verse 19).

The prodigal son's return occurs in three stages: First, he comes to himself; second, he arises; and third, he returns to his father. The Israelite prophets spoke of repentance as "returning." Viewing the prodigal's actions as repentance, biblical interpreters are quick to maintain that repentance means learning to say "Abba" again, placing one's whole trust in the heavenly Father and returning to his arms and to his house.

In verse 20, the prodigal son acts upon his resolve: He rises from the mire of the pigpen and returns to his father. Here, the parable's point of view shifts from the lost son to the awaiting father. No other image has come closer to portraying the character of God than that of the longing father, peering down the road awaiting his son's return, and then springing to his feet and running to meet him. In first-century Palestine, it was a loss of dignity for a grown man to run. Nevertheless, the father set aside superficial propriety and ran—propelled by joy and compassion—to meet his son. Significantly, the father acts exactly as the elder brother does in the patriarchal narratives of the Hebrew Scripture, "Esau ran to meet him, and embraced him, and fell on his neck and kissed him" (Genesis 33:4). The kiss is an expression of forgiveness, as when David kissed Absalom (2 Samuel 14:33).

Immediately, the son starts uttering his rehearsed speech, calling out "Father" and voicing his contrition, made all the more necessary by his father's joyful embrace. Yet, before the son can ask to return as a slave, his father interrupts him and instructs his slaves to fetch the best robe for his son's shoulders, a ring for his finger and sandals for his feet. "These are not simply festive adornments but are deeper meanings. The robe is a symbol of authority and the ring is a signet ring, so that the son can now act with the father's authority; sandals are worn only by free people; hired servants and slaves went barefoot."[7]

In publicly receiving the prodigal back into his household, the father signals the rest of the village that the boy is again to be treated as his son. He is a free man, an honored guest, a son. The lavishness of the father's acceptance is proved by his order to kill the fatted calf. The return of the prodigal son is clearly an occasion to celebrate: Meat was not part of the daily diet in first-century Palestine and was usually reserved for festivals.

In verse 24 the father sums up the significance of the first part of the story: "For this son of mine was dead and is alive again; he was lost and is found!" The son was "dead" because he had broken with the family and dishonored his father. But his return re-establishes him as his father's son. Like the sheep and the coin, once he was lost but now has been found. It was time to celebrate (verses 23–24).

## Analysis of Part Two (Luke 15:25–32)

The celebration is the impetus of the parable's second part. In verse 25, the narrative point of view shifts from the returning prodigal son to the elder son. Coming in from the fields, he learns his younger brother has returned. As he approaches the house, he hears the music and dancing. He calls one of the slaves and asks what is happening. Ingenuously, the slave answers: "Your brother has come" (15:27).

Angry, the elder brother refuses to enter the house. Again, emotional distance and physical separation signify alienation. Just as the younger son's intentions were not immediately apparent at the beginning of the story, the reason for the elder son's anger is unclear. Dramatically, the parallel continues as the father again leaves his house to meet one of his sons. Although he did not plead with his younger son, he pleads with the elder son.

Their conversation is the parable's climax. The elder son speaks first, venting his anger (verses 29–30). In contrast, every time the prodigal had spoken with his father, he respectfully addressed him as "father," even in his pigsty soliloquy (verses 12, 18 and 21). The elder son, however, refuses to acknowledge his filial and fraternal relationship. He abruptly says: "Listen!" instead of "father,"(verse 20) and likens himself to a slave—ironically, the position the prodigal had hoped to earn. Finally, he refers to his brother as "This son of yours" (verse 30) and, as proof of paternal injustice, catalogues the prodigal's filial treachery while pleading his own merits. He has worked long and hard and has never disobeyed, while the younger need only return home for the father to kill the fatted calf. Yet he as elder son has never so much as received a kid to eat in feast with his friends.

The father's response restores his family's relationships. He defends himself against his elder son's charge of injustice and justifies celebrating the prodigal's return. Despite not having been addressed as "father," the father's first word is "son" (verse 31), and it predicates all that follows: "You are always with me, and all that is mine is yours" (verse 31). Legally, because the younger son had already received his share of the patrimony, the elder son would inherit all that was left. Furthermore, the father reminds his elder son of his relationship to his brother; "this brother of yours" echoes "this son of yours" in verse 30. If repentance for the prodigal son means relearning to say "father," then, for the elder son it is relearning to say "brother."

In this parable, the celebration is necessary. If one celebrates recovering a lost sheep or coin in the two previous parables, one could hardly refuse to allow a father to celebrate the recovery of his son.

The three parables contained in the fifteenth chapter of the Gospel of Luke make their point effectively. The Pharisees and the Scribes who grumbled because Jesus broke bread with sinners are unmasked as self-serving elder sons indignantly denying their relationship with both their father (God) and brother (humanity), and refusing to join in the homecoming celebration. In the world of the parable, one cannot be a son or daughter of God without also being a brother or a sister to the children of God.

## Reflections on the Parable

This parable is a gem; each of its facets deserves considered study to reveal a textured and nuanced story.

The fascination with this parable lies in its resonance within our lives: adolescent rebellion, familial alienation, the appeal of the new and the foreign, the consequences of foolhardiness, the warmth of a home remembered, the experience of self-encounter and its consequent awakening and repentance, the joy of reunion and the power of forgiveness, the dynamics that sometimes lead brothers to part, and the contrasts between relationships based on merit and relationships based on faithful love.

Unfortunately, we usually learn to demand our rights in relationships before we learn to value our obligations. How many times, within the span of a week, will a parent hear one child say to another, "It's mine. Give it to me!"? Children quickly learn to demand their rights, but it often takes them much longer to learn to maintain relationships.

Seen from home, the "far-off country" is very appealing. Young people leave for fast living. Spouses abandon partners for liaisons with exciting new lovers. The glow of the "far-off country" is a mirage, however. Home never looks so good as when remembered from a pigsty.

The journey home begins with coming to oneself; the most difficult step is the first. The prodigal had to face himself in the pigsty of his own making before he could again face his father. Pride can keep us from admitting our mistakes; self-esteem may require us to act decisively and set right things done wrong.

Although the opportunity to remedy wrongs and restore relationships begins with coming to oneself, it requires more. We must face the person we wronged. Was the younger son merely seeking to improve his situation, or was he genuinely seeking reconciliation with his father? His interior monologue confirms his sincerity. Neither the younger son's pride nor his shame mattered as much as his need to restore his relationship with his father. He did not ask for filial privileges to be restored. He did not ask for forgiveness. He merely confessed.

A parent faces the temptation to allow an immature child's angry separation to become reciprocal. Yet, the model of parental love presented in the parable insists that no matter what the son has done he remains his father's son. When no one else would even give the prodigal food to eat, the father ran to him in acceptance. Love requires no confession and no restitution. Joyful celebration begins as soon as parent recognizes child.

Insofar as we see God's love in the waiting father's response, the parable reassures all who would confess: "Father, I have sinned against heaven and before you" (verse 18). The father's response is more than the son had dared imagine. "The parable teaches in beautiful simplicity what God is like, his limitless love, his boundless love, his amazing grace."[8] The father's celebration conveys the joy in heaven. No repentance is required; it is enough that the son has come home.

If this is the picture of God's joy in receiving a returning sinner, then it can also assure God's love to those who, facing death, wonder how they will be received. In the end, we all return home as sinners. Jesus' parable invites trust in God's goodness and mercy.

The elder son represents those of us who think we can make it on our own. Here is the contrast between those who want to live by justice and merit and those who must ask for grace. The parable shows that those who would live by merit alone can never know the joy of grace. We cannot share in the Father's grace if we demand he deal with us according to what we deserve. Sharing in God's grace requires joining in the celebration when others also receive that grace. Part of the fellowship of Christ is receiving and rejoicing with others who do not, in our view, deserve either our forgiveness or God's grace.

The parable leaves us with the open question of whether or not the elder son joined in the celebration. Did he enter the house and welcome his brother home, or did he remain outside, feeling wronged? The parable's ending is left open because this is the decision each of us must make: enter and accept the grace as the father's rule for family's life or not.

# Jesus' Feminine Images for God

Jesus imagined God as "Abba" (Mark 14:36), meaning "Daddy." He taught his disciples the prayer "Our Father." From the cross he said, "Father, into your hands I commend my spirit" (Luke 23:46). This classic masculine image for God comes from the lips of Jesus Christ in the gospels. But other images are often overlooked.

Because our tradition has overemphasized masculine images for God (king, father, shepherd, farmer), many Christians do not recognize the feminine images for God in the gospels. For example, when people hear the story of the man who sowed mustard seed, they know it is God (Matthew 13:31), but they often miss the parallel image that follows, where God is a woman, "The kingdom of heaven is like yeast that a woman took and mixed in with three measures of flour until all of it was leavened" (Matthew 13:33). Christians know that God is the shepherd in the wilderness who left his flock to search for one lost sheep (Luke 15:3–7), yet they usually do not recognize God as the woman searching for her lost coin in the passage immediately following (Luke 15:8–10).

Sometimes, Christians fail to recognize the maternal image for God when Jesus tells Nicodemus and all of us that, just as we were born physically from our mother's womb, we must be born spiritually if we wish to enter the kingdom of God (John 3:3–6).

As a storyteller, Jesus imagines God with feminine qualities and characteristics. Not only is it all right to do this, it is necessary if we wish to have a healthy, balanced image of God in our spirituality. God is spirit, neither male nor female; hence, all language about God is metaphoric.

Metaphors are tensive images, simultaneously affirmed and negated: God is our father, and is not our father; God is our mother, and is not our mother. If we forget the negating phrase "is not," we then create an idol; we make God into the image of a creature. In simultaneously holding many active metaphors for God, we remain aware that any single image is not literally true and so is inadequate to the holy mystery that is God.

# Jesus' Nature Images for God

In the gospels, Jesus draws some of his images for God from nature. For example, the word of God is a seed sown in the ground (Matthew 13:3–9; Mark 4:3–9; Luke 8:5–8); Jesus says, "I am the way, the truth, and the life" (John 14:6), and "I am the water of life" (John 4:10). These nonhuman images keep us from dividing God into three people, an idolatrous tendency that continues today. We try to fashion God in our human likeness instead of the other way around. God is not a human being. Nature images offer insight into God's nature that human images cannot.

What is the meaning of "I am the vine; you are the branches" (John 15:5)? If we observe a vine, we notice that it is almost impossible to figure out where vine ends and branch begins. With that metaphor, Jesus is saying something about the unity of life even beyond the image of husband and wife. No matter how close spouses become, they remain two distinct persons. A vine and its branches really are not two distinct things but interdependent parts of a unified whole. A vine without branches cannot bear fruit, and branches without a vine cannot survive. To say that Jesus Christ is the vine and that we are his branches underscores the interdependence between God and us in a way that a human image of God does not capture.

What is Jesus telling us when he says: "I am the living bread that came down from heaven. Whoever eats this bread will live forever" (John 6:51). Think of the food we eat. It becomes us, and we become it. If Jesus is the living bread, what does that say about our relationship with Jesus? We become part of each other we dwell within each other.

What is the significance of saying that the reign of God is like yeast in dough (Matthew 13:33)? Is that a description of conquest, with everyone forced to submit? No, that is not how leaven works. Yeast leavens gradually, transforming the dough by making it puff up without taking it over. If our sole image of the coming of the reign of God is that of Christ the conquering king, then we have a very narrow image of the reign of God and the way in which it comes about. In us, God's reign rises so that we may become food and help for the hungry and the poor, instead of exploiting conquerors.

The natural images of God in the gospels give us a different perspective on the mission of the church. They communicate things to us that cannot be expressed using human metaphors. Images such as mother, father (Matthew 6:9–13; Luke 11:2–4), shepherd (Luke 15), sower and baker (Matthew 13:3–9 and 13:33) are very useful in conveying some facets of God, but so are images such as a lamb, lamp, gate and water. We need to integrate these natural images into our Christian imagination and experience, so that they can constantly play off one another and so keep any single image from becoming an idol.

Scripture tells us God is light (Psalm 27:1) and that God is both a gentle breeze and a whirlwind (Job 38:1). God is manifest in an earthquake and fire (Exodus 3:2). God is the harvester separating the wheat from the chaff and the fisherman inspecting that day's catch. Once aware of all these images, we keep arranging and rearranging them in order to see, understand and grasp more of the divine nature than any one image can convey.

Why do Christians willingly accept the image of Christ the King as the predominant model when imagining Jesus Christ in the world (cf. Acts 17:7), but not that of Jesus as a mothering hen (Luke 13:34)? In scripture, Jesus is likened to both king and hen. Neither image is more valid, weightier or more valuable than the other. Just as it would be absurd to celebrate a feast of Christ the Hen, it would be equally absurd to celebrate the feast of Christ the King if one has in mind a sixteenth-century monarch.

For some people, the doctrine of the Holy Trinity is an obstacle to accepting the biblical images of God given us by Jesus. The Christian church developed the doctrine during the third and fourth centuries. It is a mystery no one can completely explain. In an attempt to do so, however, the doctrine that the Trinity is the Father, the Son and the Holy Spirit is reduced in the imaginations of many to the superficial image of an old man, a young man and a bird. Theological therapy for the religious imagination is needed.

First, God is *not* three people, much less three men. God is the one, the Holy Mystery in whom we live and move and have our being (cf. Acts 17:28). We experience God according to our limited capacities, under various *personae* ("actors masks" in both Greek and Latin). We experience God as the divine origin, source or ground of our being; as the divine communicator and communication; as redeemer; as divine energy; as the one who makes us holy by enlivening us with God's own life. The use of biblical language for God—such as creator and parent, word and wisdom, spirit and breath of life—helps express our human experiences of God.

Jesus' addressing God with the Aramaic word *Abba,* daddy (Mark 14:36), canonized the use of father language to designate the first person of the Trinity, even though Jesus also used feminine images for God. God is not literally a father nor are the the possibilities for imagining the second person of the Trinity exhausted solely by the image of son. Jesus claimed to be the Wisdom of God, a feminine personification from the Hebrew Scriptures (cf. Wisdom 8:22—9:18).

Because Jesus was a man, his experience of being a child of God was that of being a son, not that of being a daughter. When Christianity came to understand Jesus Christ as incarnation of both Word *(logos)* and Wisdom *(sophia),* the word "Son" was applied to the second person of the Trinity. For theologically sound spirituality, Christians need the solidity of monotheistic faith—one God, not three— wherein God is experienced through many metaphors, masculine and feminine, human and nonhuman.

Finally, one moves beyond spoken, written and imagistic metaphors into the brilliant darkness of mystical experience where God, who is pure spirit and ultimate mystery, is unconfined by metaphors. In his book, *The Idea of the Holy*,[9] Rudolph Otto called God the *mysterium tremendum et fascinans*, the mystery that simultaneously fascinates and frightens. These dual feelings about God give us pause and helps us understand that God is beyond imagination.

# Father

Having said this, we need to wrestle with the fact that when Jesus teaches his disciples to pray, he refers specifically to God as father (Matthew 6:9–13 and Luke 11:2–4). The gospels tell of Jesus using the word *father* in his own dialogue with God. In addition, Jesus assured his disciples that because of their relation with and faith in him, they too could call God *Abba* (John 20:17). In view of the Hebrew scriptures' reluctance to use this familiar title for God, its use by Jesus manifests his intimacy with God. Initiating his disciples into that intimacy was his great gift to them. The father Jesus gave us, however, was also mother, friend, the One who sends, the great "I Am." Father is not an exclusive image for God, though it is that one that understandably became especially dear to the first Christians. The word *father*, as title of address for God, has been over-stressed and needs to be balanced with other images.

# The Reign of God

Corollary to this matter is the phrase "the kingdom of God." According to the gospels, Jesus says, "The time is fulfilled and the kingdom of God has come near" (Mark 1:15).

Many scholars prefer to translate "kingdom of God" as "reign of God."[10] That interpretation helps break the stranglehold that male monarchism has had on our religious imagination. The image of the reign of God dates to the Hebrew Scriptures, where God talks of being the king of Israel. That image is meant as a check on human kings, reminding them who is truly in control. God in effect says, "Don't ever get it into your royal heads, Solomon and company, that you are in charge. Because if you do, the day will come when the Babylonians will defeat you. Then you will know that it is not by your power, your horses and your chariots but by my loving providence that anything is accomplished."

The term "reign of God" stresses the presence of God's justice at work. The "reign of God" is the human circumstance in which the love, justice and mercy of God control all relationships and govern all human affairs. It does not have a power structure in which God's representatives rule. It is not a time when armies will go forth to conquer and convert everyone to Christianity. The "reign of God" is a time of universal well-being in which human structures, relationships and society will be centered on love and justice. Therefore, the "reign of God" is in you and me. It is among us. It is operating wherever the Spirit of God is at work.

So, the "reign of God" is meant to serve as contrast to human kingship; it is meant to keep human monarchs from arrogance. A similar contrast is evoked when God is called "father" in the gospels. The image of God as father opposes the authoritarian, patriarchal image wherein the father is the family's "little king." Jesus shows that such an image is not about divine paternity, the fatherhood of God is about infinite forgiveness, like that offered to a prodigal child. It's about the gift of life, and love that has nothing to do with domination.

Images of God as king and father are meant to correct perverted human realities, but people have used them to legitimize human patriarchy in the name of God. For that reason, the metaphors of king and father have acquired an undeserved aura of divinity rather than being seen as images for God.

# Conclusion

From this brief survey of Jesus' images for God, we can conclude that along with natural images, Jesus provides feminine and masculine images for God. The many and varied images that the gospels contain provide a basis for the many images that many Christians today use for God. Despite this our language remains limited when we reflect upon God.

Jesus the icon and storyteller of God encourages us to wrestle with the mystery that is God by recognizing that God is one, and that God is spirit, not physical, and by recognizing that the parables of the good shepherd, the lost coin and the prodigal son are all revelations about God.

# For Discussion

1. For you, who besides Jesus Christ is an icon of God?

2. What do you mean when you say "Jesus is the Son of God"? Explain.

3. Aside from the examples in this chapter, are there any other parables in the gospels that provide you with images for God?

4. Of all the images for God presented by Jesus in this chapter, which one is your favorite? Why?

# Biblical Images for the Holy Spirit

When you send forth your Spirit,
they are created;
and you renew the face of the ground.

(Psalm 104:30)

It is difficult to say anything about a spirit. Its very nature is ethereal, elusive and uncontained. It defies the physical considerations that keep the rest of us earthbound. A spirit is as difficult to grasp as a breath of fresh air, which is, coincidentally, how we got our first glimmer of understanding of the Holy Spirit in biblical revelation.

# Chapter Five

73

# Spirit as the Breath of God

*Ruach*, the Hebrew word for spirit, also denotes "breath," "wind" and "moving air." *Ruach* is a dynamic entity through which God achieves divine purposes. It is the principle of life and power.

The phrase *ruach elohim*, "spirit of God," occurs in the Hebrew Scriptures 94 times, mostly in connection to God's power and creation and to God's animating Israel's leaders. Scholar Elizabeth Johnson notes that. "Spirit, literally meaning a blowing wind, a storm, a stream of air, breath in motion, or something dynamically in movement and impossible to pin down, points to the livingness of God who creates, sustains and guides all things and cannot be confined."[11]

The "spirit of God," also translated as "a mighty wind" and "a wind from God," sweeps over the waters and initiates creation: "The earth was a formless void and darkness covered the face of the deep, while a wind from God swept [hovered] over the face of the waters" (Genesis 1:2). It is this wind, God's breath, that brings order to chaos so that creation may begin. The Hebrew word used for *hovered* is the same word used for a bird as it hovers while teaching its chick to leave the nest and learn to fly.

In Genesis 1:2, the Spirit of God is the creative, life-giving and sustaining presence of God. This same notion is also found in Psalm 104, which describes the dependence of all life, human and animal, upon God: "These all look to you, to give them food in due season" (Psalm 104:27). Verse 30 highlights the Spirit's role:

> When you send forth your Spirit they are created;
> and you renew the face of the ground. (Psalm 104:30)

In Ezekiel, the Spirit of God is the giver of life in the vision of the valley of dry bones. The reassembled bones are lifeless until the Spirit enters them:

> Then he said to me, "Prophesy to the breath, prophesy, mortal, and say to the breath: Thus says the Lord God: Come from the four winds, O breath, and breathe upon these slain, that they might live." I prophesied as he commanded me, and the breath came into them, and they lived, and stood on their feet, a vast multitude. (Ezekiel 37:9–10)

Psalms 51 and 139 make it clear that the Spirit is the equivalent of the all-encompassing, life-giving presence of God:

> Do not cast me away from your presence,
> and do not take your holy spirit from me. (Psalm 51:11)

> Where can I go from your spirit?
> Or where can I flee from your presence? (Psalm 139:7)

In these verses, the words *presence* and *spirit* are parallels. Wherever the spirit is, so is God, and vice-versa.

In the second story of creation God gives breath, spirit, the power of life, to created beings: "The Lord God formed man from the dust of the ground, and breathed into his nostrils the breath of life; and man became a living being" (Genesis 2:7).

It is the Spirit of God that creates and sustains life: "The spirit of God has made me, and the breath of the Almighty gives me life" (Job 33:4). The prophet Isaiah recalls creation, proclaiming: "Thus says God . . . who gives breath to the people upon it [earth] and spirit [wind] to those who walk in it" (Isaiah 42:5). So says Zechariah in his oracles: "Thus says the Lord, who stretched out the heavens and founded the earth and formed the human spirit within" (Zechariah 12:1). Thus, the Spirit of God is first represented in scripture as the gift of life manifest in the images of breath and wind—in other words, life is the gift of God.[2]

# The Spirit as Surprise

In addition to the Spirit's presence in people as the ordinary gift of life, the Spirit also comes as a surprise, a divine intrusion into the life of human beings. One way the Spirit of God manifested itself as surprise was in the ancient Israelite leaders—Moses, the judges, kings and prophets—whom God raised to lead in time of crisis.

The Spirit, who is God's "mover" throughout the Bible, impels Moses to lead his people out of slavery and forge them into a new nation. At each critical turn in the story of its salvation the Spirit raises new servants of God to lead the nation.

In one such crisis, the Israelites, no longer content with daily manna, began complaining. Seeing that Moses would need help, God orders him to gather 70 of the elders of Israel and take them out of the camp and to the tent of meeting. God tells Moses, "I will take some of the spirit that is on you and put it on them; and they shall bear the burden of the people along with you so that you will not bear it all by yourself" (Numbers 11:17).

This account becomes more intriguing as it progresses because it illuminates the dimension of surprise and reinforces the idea that the Spirit's activity cannot be confined or predicted. After God instills some of Moses' spirit into the group of elders, they discover that two others, Eldad and Medad, had remained in camp instead of joining the meeting in the tent. Nevertheless, the Spirit came upon them, and they began prophesying among the people in the camp. Annoyed by this, an assistant to Moses complains: "My lord Moses, stop them." Moses retorts: "Are you jealous for my sake? Would that all the Lord's people were prophets and that the Lord could put his spirit on them!" (Numbers 11:28–29). This passage teaches that no one can control God's Spirit; it will reside in whomever God chooses.

# The Spirit of God and Israel's Leaders

The Hebrew Scriptures are replete with exciting examples of the Spirit of God coming upon the heroes of Israel. The Spirit of God raises up Judges: Othneal (Judges 3:10), Gideon (Judges 6:34) and Samson (Judges 13:25; 14:6 and 19; 15:14). The Spirit of God helps Samson act beyond his ordinary powers: "The spirit of the Lord rushed on him and he tore the lion apart bare-handed as one might tear apart a kid " (Judges 14:6). The Spirit of the Lord also rushes upon the new king Saul after Samuel anoints him (cf. 1 Samuel 11:6). On another occasion, God told Samuel to fill his horn with oil and anoint the shepherd boy David who was destined to become a great king of Israel and an ancestor of Jesus. When Samuel anoints him, "the spirit of the Lord came upon David from that day forward" (1 Samuel 16:13). The Spirit of God quietly possesses David and remains with him, a good example of how, even today, the Spirit takes over the lives of many servants of God.

# The Spirit of God and the Prophets

The biblical prophets are one group in whom the Spirit of God is very active. Their mission is to communicate God's revelation and message to the people.

It is by the Spirit of God that the prophet Balaam, a foreigner, utters his oracles (Numbers 24:2)[3], demonstrating that God's Spirit was not limited to the Israelite prophets. King Saul joins a group of prophets in their prophetic state when the spirit of God rushes upon him (1 Samuel 10:6 and 10). David's last words are uttered through the Spirit of God (2 Samuel 23:2), and in the book of Kings the Spirit carries off Elijah (1 Kings 18:12; 2 Kings 2:16). Isaiah prophesies: "The spirit of the Lord God is upon me, because the Lord has anointed me; he has sent me to bring good news to the oppressed, to bind up the brokenhearted, to proclaim liberty to the captives, and release to the prisoners" (Isaiah 61:1; cf. Luke 4:18). Ezekiel recounts how God called him to prophesy to Israel: "And when [God] spoke to me, the spirit entered into me and set me on my feet" (Ezekiel 2:2; cf. Micah 3:8). Ezra recalls that when Israel was rebellious, "you were patient with them for many years, bearing witness against them through your spirit, by means of your prophets" (Nehemiah 9:30; similarly Zechariah 7:12).

Joel promises an outpouring of the Spirit upon humanity in the messianic age: "Your sons and daughters shall prophesy. . . . Even upon the servants and the handmaids, in those days, I will pour out my spirit" (Joel 2:28). Isaiah also prophesied the pouring out of the Spirit on the whole people in the messianic age (Isaiah 32:15). Similarly, Zechariah declares, "And I will pour out a spirit of compassion and supplication on the house of David and the inhabitants of Jerusalem" (Zechariah 12:10; cf. Ezekiel 39:29).

Ezekiel spoke to the exiles of God's renewal of Israel: "I will give them a new heart and put a new spirit within them" (Ezekiel 11:19), and "A new heart I will give you and a new spirit I will put within you" (Ezekiel 36:26). Thus the people will again be able to live according to God's statutes. Israel, however, must respond to God's action and make for themselves "a new heart and a new spirit" (Ezekiel 18:31). In Ezekiel's vision, God says to the bones: "I will cause breath [wind, spirit] to enter you, and you shall live" (37:5). Though covered with sinew and flesh, the bones come alive only when entered by the Spirit of God (37:10), "I will put my spirit in you that you may live" (37:14).

In Ezekiel, the Spirit is presented as an educator. The English verb to *educate* is derived from the Latin word *educare*, "to lead out." Although most prophets were drawn into the divine sphere by the Spirit that filled and possessed them, Ezekiel is led, lifted and carried away by the Spirit of God. It enters him (cf. Ezekiel 2:2). These texts bear witness to the Spirit's important role in the life and ministry of Ezekiel:

The spirit lifted me up and bore me away. (Ezekiel 3:14)

The spirit lifted me up and brought me to the east gate. (Ezekiel 11:1)

The spirit lifted me up and brought me in a vision by the spirit of God into Chaldea, to the exiles. (Ezekiel 11:24)

In Ezekiel, the Spirit's activity is educational. It leads him out with prophetic visions of the future of his defeated people. Ezekiel lived closer to the time of the exile than did the other prophets and may have witnessed the destruction of his people and their land. Through visions, the Spirit teaches Ezekiel that the future is open and that God's covenant with Israel is not past. There is a community yet to be and a temple to be created.

These texts show how important the role of God's Spirit was in the life and ministry of the biblical prophets. It was the very life force of God that supported and stood behind the prophets and their message.

In the Hebrew Scriptures God's empowering Spirit is passed from one leader to the next. Upon Moses' death, "Joshua, son of Nun, was filled with the spirit of wisdom, since Moses had laid his hand upon him" (Deuteronomy 34:9). When the Spirit of God comes upon the newly anointed king David, it departs from Saul (1 Samuel 16:13–14). When Elisha succeeds Elijah, he requests from him "a double portion of your spirit" (2 Kings 2:9), and when Elijah is taken to heaven in a whirlwind, the guild prophets remark, "The spirit of Elijah rests on Elisha" (2 Kings 2:15).

# The Spirit of God as Bird

In the Hebrew Scriptures, another image for the Spirit of God is the bird. As discussed before, the Spirit is seen as a bird hovering encouragingly above its chick, teaching it to fly. The Spirit of God hovers like a nesting bird over the primordial chaos at creation (Genesis 1:2). Like a mother bird, God shelters the troubled:

Guard me as the apple of your eye; hide me in the shadow of your wings. (Psalm 17:8)

All people take refuge in the shadow of your wings. (Psalm 36:7)

In the shadow of your wings I will take refuge, until the destroying storms pass by. (Psalm 57:1)

Let me abide in your tent forever, find refuge under the shelter of your wings. (Psalm 61:4)

You who live in the shelter of the Most High, who abide in the shadow of the Almighty. (Psalm 91:1)

In summary, the Spirit image contained in the Hebrew Scriptures is conceived as a dynamic divine entity by which God's purposes are realized. The Spirit is the source of life, a creative and charismatic power. Its origin and its course, like the very mystery of God, cannot be discovered. Hence, to the Spirit of God are attributed the effects of actions humans find mysterious.

# The Spirit in the New Testament

The Christian Scriptures were originally written in Greek. The Greek word *pneuma*, "spirit," is similar in meaning and usage to the Hebrew word *ruach*. It is a movement of air, primarily breath or wind, which may signify a life-giving element. When the adjective *holy* is attached, the reference is to the divine Spirit of God.

There are instances of the use of *pneuma* to signify evil spirits. This is usual in Mark's gospel. It also denotes the life principle which leaves the body at death (Matthew 27:50). Often the Spirit and the flesh are contrasted; the Spirit is strong and willing, while the flesh is weak and yielding (Matthew 26:41; Mark 14:38). These uses of the word will not be treated here; we will focus on the use of the word as an image of God.

The Spirit as image of divine power is a common concept in the New Testament. The Spirit is the power that drives Jesus into the desert (Mark 1:12) and the power with which he expels demons (Matthew 12:28). It is the power that inspires the writers of the Christian Scriptures (cf. Matthew 22:43; Mark 12:36 and Hebrews 4).

In the infancy narratives of both Matthew (1:18–20) and Luke (1:35), the conception of Jesus is attributed to the Holy Spirit. The spirit is given to Jesus in baptism (Matthew 3:13–17; Mark 1:9–11; Luke 3:21–22; John 1:29–34). The spirit is also given to the disciples of Jesus (John 20:22) and will speak in them when they are called upon to bear witness (Matthew 24:20; Mark 13:11).

# The Spirit and the Gospel of John

## The Story of Jesus and Nicodemus

In the Gospel of John the conversation between Jesus and Nicodemus, includes a maternal metaphor for the Spirit of God. Jesus insists that a person must be born anew in order to enter the reign of God. Nicodemus asks: "How can anyone be born after having grown old? Can one enter a second time into the mother's womb and be born?" (John 3:4).

Jesus' reply retains the birth metaphor and expands upon it in speaking of being born of God: "Very truly, I tell you, no one can enter the kingdom of God without being born of water and spirit. What is born of the flesh is flesh, and what is born of the Spirit is spirit" (John 3:5–6). Therefore, if a person desires to move from life's natural level to its divine level, it is God who must do the raising. Just as God did in the creation when instilling the Spirit into humanity's lifeless form, the new gift of life must be communicated through the divine Spirit. Jesus communicates this life-giving Spirit because he is the heavenly Son of Man who descended from heaven (John 3:13).

## The Role of the Paraclete in John's Gospel

In the Gospel of John, the Spirit of God is further identified as the Paraclete; some translations use the term *counselor* or *advocate*.[4] "The Greek word *paracletos* means "one called to the side of another" much like an attorney who stands with someone in a court of law. In John's gospel, Jesus promises the Paraclete to his disciples five times:

> And I will ask the Father, and he will give you another Advocate, to be with you forever. This is the Spirit of truth, whom the world cannot receive, because it neither sees him nor knows him. You know him, because he abides with you, and he will be in you. (John 14:16–17)

> But the Advocate, the Holy Spirit, whom the Father will send in my name, will teach you everything, and remind you of all that I have said to you. (John 14:26)

> When the Advocate comes, whom I will send to you from the Father, the Spirit of truth who comes from the Father, he will testify on my behalf. (John 15:26)

> Nevertheless I tell you the truth: it is to your advantage that I go away, for if I do not go away, the Advocate will not come to you; but if I go, I will send him to you. And when he comes, he will prove the world wrong about sin and righteousness and judgment: about sin, because they do not believe in me; about righteousness, because I am going to the Father and you will see me no longer; about judgment, because the ruler of this world has been condemned. (John 16:7–11)

When the Spirit of truth comes, he will guide you into all the truth; for he will not speak on his own, but will speak whatever he hears, and he will declare to you the things that are to come. He will glorify me, because he will take what is mine and declare it to you. All that the Father has is mine. For this reason, I said that he will take what is mine and declare it to you. (John 16:13–15)

As the fourth gospel makes clear, the Paraclete is the Holy Spirit, the Spirit of Truth (John 14:17 and 26). The Paraclete has important post-resurrection roles: The Paraclete will be the personal presence of Jesus Christ after his death and subsequent absence from history; as the "Spirit of Truth," it is understood to abide with the disciples, teaching, maintaining and completing the work of Jesus while leading them to all truths (John 16:13); and, in the Gospel of John, the Paraclete is the prosecutor and judge, convicting the world for its sins of hatred and unbelief (John 16:7–11).

For John's gospel, all was made possible by the presence of the one Spirit. In a confusing and complex world, the Spirit of God will guide all followers of Jesus. As Jesus taught and protected them, so too will the Paraclete guide the disciples.

The fourth gospel's genius is its specific insights into the Paraclete's nature and function. The Paraclete comes from and is related to both the Father and the Son, and will come only at Jesus Christ's departure (John 17:7; 15:26). The Father sends the Paraclete in response to Jesus' request (John 14:16). The Paraclete is sent in the name of Jesus (John 14:26) and is also called the "Spirit of Truth" (cf. John 14:17; 15:26; 16:13). The Paraclete is synonymous with the Holy Spirit (John 14:26) and is also called "another Paraclete," indirectly implying that Jesus also is a Paraclete (John 14:16).

The Paraclete has a relationship with the disciples of Jesus as well as with the world. The Paraclete remains with the disciples and will be recognized by them (John 14:16–17). The Paraclete teaches them (16:13), announces the future (16:13) and declares what does and does not belong to Jesus (16:14), all while glorifying and giving witness to Jesus (15:26; 16:14). Reminding the disciples of all Jesus said (14:26), the Paraclete speaks only what is heard and not of his own authority (John 16:13).

The world cannot see, recognize or accept the Paraclete (14:17), and, in that rejection, the Paraclete is witness to Jesus (15:18–26), proving the world guilty of sin and deserving of condemnation (16:8–11).

For John's gospel, the presence of the Paraclete resolves the question of the delay in the Second Coming of Jesus Christ, because the Paraclete is Jesus. Thus, Jesus has returned and is present in the community.

The Paraclete preserves the revelation of God in Jesus Christ for future generations by teaching only what Jesus taught. The Paraclete joins future generations of Christians in the ministry, death and resurrection of Jesus Christ.

Finally, near the end of the Gospel of John, Jesus gives the spirit to his disciples: "Jesus said to them again, 'Peace be with you. As the Father has sent me, so I send you.' When he had said this, he breathed on them and said to them, 'Receive the Holy Spirit' " (John 20:21–22). In this passage, Jesus acts like the Spirit, the breath of God that hovered over the waters and over Adam when God created humankind. Jesus' new breath of creation is over the disciples, giving them God's holy breath, bringing order to their lives and empowering them to become church.

# The Holy Spirit in the Gospel of Luke

The Gospel of Luke is known as the gospel of the Holy Spirit. From Luke, the Holy Spirit receives more recognition than from any other evangelist.[5] The expression "Holy Spirit" appears 13 times in the Gospel of Luke, and 41 times in the Acts of the Apostles, written by the same author.

From the beginning of the Gospel of Luke, the Holy Spirit plays an essential role. Zechariah is told that his son, John, will "even before his birth be filled with the Holy Spirit." (Luke 1:15). Jesus is said to have originated from the Holy Spirit. The angel tells Mary: "The Holy Spirit will come upon you and the power of the Most High will overshadow you" (Luke 1:35). When Mary visits Elizabeth, the evangelist notes that "Elizabeth was filled with the Holy Spirit" (Luke 1:41). Why? Because Mary, who is pregnant with Jesus, transfers God's Spirit to John and his mother, Elizabeth. In Luke's gospel, even the unborn Jesus bears the Spirit of God to everyone he encounters.

Once Zechariah, the father of John the Baptist, regains his speech, he prophesies about the meaning of his son's birth. Luke points out that John's "father, Zechariah, was filled with the Holy Spirit" as he began his canticle, the *Benedictus*, "Blessed be the Lord God of Israel" (Luke 1:67).

In the story of the presentation of Jesus in the Temple, found only in the Gospel of Luke, the aged Simeon is said to have had the Holy Spirit rest on him (Luke 2:25). Luke continues:

> It had been revealed to [Simeon] by the Holy Spirit that he would not see death before he had seen the Lord's Messiah. Guided by the spirit, Simeon came into the temple; and when the parents brought in the child Jesus, . . . Simeon took him in his arms and praised God. (Luke 2:26–27)

Of course, this is followed by Simeon's canticle, the *Nunc Dimitis*, "Master, now you are dismissing your servant in peace, according to your word."

Jesus is preeminently the man of the Holy Spirit and the giver of the spirit in the Gospel of Luke. Identifying Jesus as the Spirit's living conduit, John the Baptist says: "I baptize you with water; but one who is more powerful than I is coming. . . . He will baptize you with the Holy Spirit and fire" (Luke 3:16).

A pivotal point in Jesus' life, as portrayed in the Gospel of Luke, is his baptism. Too often we have skimmed over this event as if it were a mere formality, but the scene vibrates with meaning:

Now when all the people were baptized, and when Jesus also had been baptized and was praying, the heaven was opened, and the Holy Spirit descended upon him in bodily form like a dove. And the voice came from heaven, 'You are my son, the beloved; with you I am well pleased.' (Luke 3:21–22)

In the baptism of Jesus, it is clear that the Holy Spirit descends upon him in the form of a dove. Why a dove? The dove is the sign of a new season in the Song of Songs, which exclaims, "The flowers appear on the earth; the time of singing has come, and the voice of the turtle dove is heard in our land"(Song of Solomon 2:12). The dove also heralds the new world after the flood (Genesis 8:8–12). Therefore, its presence at Jesus' baptism suggests the beginning of a new age.

From Genesis 1:2, we recall that the Hebrew verb describing God's Spirit at creation also describes a bird's hovering above its nest and inciting its nestlings to fly. Such was the meaning of the Spirit of God hovering above primeval waters at the opening of the ages and above the flood waters that closed the old age and opened a new one. The dove heralded the new age begun in the story of Noah and a new season in the Song of Solomon. Surely, the Holy Spirit's descent upon Jesus as a dove suggests the introduction of both a new creation and a new age.

According to the Gospel of Luke, the Holy Spirit was in charge of the life, ministry and world of Jesus from the moment of his baptism. Thereafter, what Jesus spoke was what the Father revealed and communicated to him through and in the Spirit. Hence, the deeds of Jesus were likewise regulated, determined and made meaningful through the Spirit of God.

For Luke, the baptism of Jesus is God's decisive intervention in our history. In the Jordan River Jesus saw and experienced the Holy Spirit and, under its auspices, began his ministry. In the power of the Spirit, Jesus was driven into the wilderness and in its power returned to Galilee (Luke 4:1–14).

Further, Luke is clear that Jesus brought the Spirit of God. In fact, when Jesus begins his ministry, he stands in the synagogue in Nazareth and applies Isaiah's prophetic words to himself: "The Spirit of the Lord is upon me, because he has anointed me to bring good news to the poor. He has sent me to proclaim release to the captives and recovery of sight to the blind, to let the oppressed go free, to proclaim the year of the Lord's favor" (Luke 4:18–19).

In this passage, Luke sees Jesus as God's anointed. The Hebrew word *messiah* and its Greek equivalent, *Christos,* mean "God's anointed." In the Hebrew Scriptures *messiah* is a kingly title because prophets often anointed kings (Saul and David were both anointed by Samuel). Just as the olive oil used in anointing penetrated the skin, so too did God's Spirit penetrate the anointed. The gospels understood that Jesus was completely penetrated with God's Spirit. In the Gospel of Luke the crucified and dying Jesus says, "Father, into your hands I commend my spirit" (Luke 23:46).

# The Holy Spirit and Pentecost

In the second chapter of the Acts of the Apostles, is the marvelous story of Pentecost:

> When the day of Pentecost had come, they were all together in one place. And suddenly from heaven there came a sound like the rush of a violent wind, and it filled the entire house where they were sitting. Divided tongues, as of fire, appeared among them, and a tongue rested on each of them. All of them were filled with the Holy Spirit and began to speak in other languages, as the Spirit gave them ability.
>
> Now there were devout Jews from every nation under heaven living in Jerusalem. And at this sound the crowd gathered and was bewildered, because each one heard them speaking in the native language of each. Amazed and astonished, they asked, "Are not all these who are speaking Galileans? And how is it that we hear, each of us, in our own native language? Parthians, Medes, Elamites, and residents of Mesopotamia, Judea and Cappadocia, Pontus and Asia, Phrygia and Pamphylia, Egypt and the parts of Libya belonging to Cyrene, and visitors from Rome, both Jews and proselytes, Cretans and Arabs—in our own languages we hear them speaking about God's deeds of power." All were amazed and perplexed, saying to one another, "What does this mean?" (Acts 2:1–12)

Luke's description of the outpouring of the Holy Spirit upon the early church conveys the early church's deep conviction that theirs was a Spirit-impelled church.

Only Luke describes the descent of the Holy Spirit as occurring on the Feast of Pentecost. He does this to help his readers understand the gift of the Spirit. In Jewish tradition, the Feast of Pentecost celebrated two things: the gift of the Covenant and the gift of the Torah, the law. Both were received at Mount Sinai amid fire and wind, storm clouds and thunder. In fact, the writings of Philo Judaeus and and other Jewish contemporaries of Luke associated fire and wind with the Jewish Feast of Pentecost.

Luke is saying that the the new covenant and the new law are not written in stone but in the heart. It is the new covenant of the Spirit promised by Ezekiel: "A new heart I will give you, and a new spirit I will put within you; and I will remove from your body the heart of stone and give you a heart of flesh. I will put my spirit within you and make you follow my statutes and be careful to observe my ordinances" (Ezekiel 36:26–27). Or, as the prophet Jeremiah said: "But this is the covenant I will make with the house of Israel after those days, says the Lord: I will put my law within them, and I will write it on their hearts; and I will be their God, and they shall be my people" (Jeremiah 31:33).

Any first-century Jewish convert to Christianity would read the account of Pentecost in Acts and say: "Well, the final covenant of the Spirit of God and the final law are now given. Because all the things our tradition has told us about the covenant and the law and about what God is going to do in the final times when he pours out his Spirit have happened!"

Luke's account of Pentecost offers a vision of universal unity, a forecast of what will happen when the church and the apostles move out into the nations of the earth. There will be one message, a mystery of unity and diversity, reaching all the nations of earth in tongues under heaven.

Three times in the text, Luke writes, "*Each one heard them* [plural] speaking in his own language." If each one heard members of other language groups speaking one's language, then it was not just a miracle of speaking but also a miracle of *hearing;* the curse of the Tower of Babel has been reversed.

The story of the Tower of Babel, in Genesis 11, is the climax of the sequence of evil caused by Adam and Eve in their rejection of the source of their life: alienation from God and nature (expulsion from Paradise), familial disunity (Cain's murder of Abel, the flood, and now humanity's disunity at Babel). At Pentecost, humanity's original unity is restored through the power of the Spirit. That Luke alludes to the Tower of Babel story in the Pentecost account is clear from his playing with the word *confused,* the same word used to describe the confusion of languages at the building of the Tower of Babel. One interesting inversion in Luke's allusion is that the crowds at Babel were confused because their one language had been fragmented into many, but now people are confused all over again because they all hear the one message and understand.

# The Spirit: Feminine Life-Giver

A growing number of men and women theologians use the third person feminine pronoun *she* in speaking of the Spirit of God. Three scriptural references suggest why.

First, as already noted, the English word *spirit* is a translation of the feminine Hebrew noun *ruach*, meaning air, wind or breath. It is the word for the hovering wind in creation (Genesis 1:2) and for God's breath giving life to humanity (Genesis 2:7).

Second, the Gospel of Luke explicitly states that the Spirit descended upon Jesus "in bodily form like a dove" (Luke 3:22). Luke may have emphasized the dove as the material manifestation of the Spirit of God so that his Gentile audience could and would grasp the image's feminine nature, since in his world the dove also was a symbol for goddesses such as Astarte in Phoenicia, Athene in Greece, and Venus in Rome.

Third, in the Book of Revelation, John has a vision of a "river of life-giving water . . . flowing from the throne of God and of the Lamb. . . . On either side of the river grew the tree of life that produces fruit twelve times a year" (Revelation 22:1–2). This life-giving river is an image for the Holy Spirit. It calls to mind the life giving waters of John's Gospel, also an image for the Holy Spirit (cf. John 7:38–39). The river is a symbol of fertility, and in John's culture goddesses were the agents of fertility.

Although words and images drawn from human experience cannot describe God either accurately or completely, the writers of scripture evidently perceived the feminine qualities in the person and mission of the Holy Spirit.

# For Discussion

1. Do you ever breathe and think your breath comes from and is part of God's breath?

2. Do you ever feel that God's Spirit inspires you, as were the prophets?

3. In your life, are there key moments where the Holy Spirit has been present? Please Explain.

4. What does it mean for you to be "born again of water and the Spirit?"

5. What are some of the ways in which you can release the power of the spirit?

# Epilogue

The Bible does not provide us with only one way of speaking about God, nor does it offer a single name or image for God. Throughout this book, we have explored the Sacred Scriptures, "the texts of mystery" that reflect upon and wrestle with the mystery of God. Our study and reflections show that within the Bible, language and imagery about God are always multivalent. No language about God, not even biblical language, will ever adequately articulate the awesome, burning mystery that is God. What is inspiring and revelatory about the Bible is its posture of humility and reverence—not fear—in the presence of the deity. This is well articulated by the prophet Zephaniah when he advises everyone to "Be silent before the Lord God!" (Zephaniah 1:7). Meaning not only cessation of speech but also of written language in God's presence. In doing so, one may have an encounter with God.

I hope this book has helped widen your language about God and broaden your spectrum of metaphors and images for God. I hope it has rekindled your desire to read, study, and pray from and with the Bible. Most of all, I hope it has helped rekindle intimacy, awe, wonder and humility in your relationship with God, so that, like the prophet Amos and the people in the Bible, you can better "prepare to meet your God" (Amos 4:12).

# Endnotes

## Chapter One

1 John T. Pawlikowski. "Jews and Christians: The Contemporary Dialogue," *Quarterly Review* 4 (Winter 1984), 26–27. Similar sentiments were shared by the late Joseph Cardinal Bernardin; see "A Cardinal Looks at 25 Years of Jewish-Catholic Relations" *Proceedings of the Center for Jewish-Christian Learning*, 4 (1989), 35–37. For further reading on the topic of "Hebrew Scriptures" versus "Old Testament," see Michael Shermis and Arthur E. Zannoni, editors, *Introduction to Jewish-Christian Relations* (Mahwah, N.J.: Paulist Press, 1991), 7–33.

2 *Catechism of the Catholic Church* (New York: William H. Sadlier, Inc., 1994), 17.

3 Elizabeth A. Johnson, *She Who Is* (New York: Crossroad, 1994), 116.

4 William J. Bausch. *A World of Stories for Preachers and Teachers* (Mystic, Connecticut: Twenty Third Publications, 1998), 337.

## Chapter Two

1 Brian Wren, *What Language Shall I Borrow? God-Talk in Worship: A Male Response to Feminist Theology* (New York: Crossroads, 1995), 61.

2 Phyllis Trible, *God and the Rhetoric of Sexuality* (Philadelphia: Fortress, 1978), 18.

3 Ibid., 21.

4 Baruch A. Levine, *Leviticus (The JPS Torah Commentary)* (Philadelphia, New York and Jerusalem: The Jewish Publication Society, 1989), 256.

5 Ibid., 256.

6 Martin Buber, *The Prophetic Faith* (New York: Macmillan, 1949), 164.

7 Martin Buber, *Moses—The Revelation and the Covenant* (New York: Harper & Row, 1958), 52.

8 The title *Yahweh Sabaoth* should be mentioned here. This compound name, meaning "Lord of Hosts" or "Lord of the Armies" occurs 279 times in the Hebrew Scriptures and depicts God as a military commander. Originating in holy war, the expression became a polemic against astral cults: Yahweh rules the heavenly armies. Eventually, the name was understood as "Lord Almighty," a plural of intensity neutralizing the existence of celestial gods. The Septuagint, which is the Greek translation of the Hebrew text for Greek-speaking Jews, translates

the name *Yahweh Sabaoth* as "Lord Almighty." For further reading, see B.W. Anderson, "God, Names of," in *Interpreter's Dictionary of the Bible,* ed. G. Buttrick (Nashville: Abingdon, 1962), 407–417.

9 Buber, Martin, *Moses—The Revelation and the Covenant,* 52.

10 John Courtney Murray. *The Problem of God* (New Haven: Yale University, 1964), 16.

11 Ibid., 23.

12 For a further explanation of Israel's understanding of covenant and God's role in it, see Arthur E. Zannoni, "Bonding with God: The Biblical Covenant," *Catechumenate* 21 (May 1999), 2–9.

# Chapter Three

1 Arthur E. Zannoni, "Bonding with God: the Biblical Covenant," *Catechumenate* 21 (May 1999): 6.

2 Before the development of a sensitivity for ecumenical and interreligious dialogue, Christians dated everything either BC (Before Christ) or AD *(Anno Domini,* "The year of our Lord"). More recently, to respect all sensibilities, scholars began using the terms BCE (Before the Common Era) and CE (Common Era). The Common Era refers to the historical time period Jews and Christians share in common.

3 Elizabeth A. Johnson, *She Who Is: The Mystery of God in Feminist Theological Discourse* (New York: Crossroad, 1992), 90.

4 Roland. E Murphy, *Tree of Life: An Exposition of Biblical Wisdom Literature* (New York: Doubleday, 1990), 133.

5 J.M. McKay, "Psalms of Vigil," *Zeitschrift fur die Altestantliche Wissenschaft* 91 (1979):232–37.

6 See the note in the *New American Bible* on Exodus 23:15; B.S. Childs, *The Book of Exodus* (Old Testament Library; Philadelphia: Westminster Press, 1972), 451.

# Chapter Four

1 Marcus Borg, *Meeting Jesus Again for the First Time* (San Francisco: Harper), 1994; 102.

2 Elizabeth A. Johnson. *She Who Is: The Mystery of God in Feminist Theological Discourse* (New York: Crossroad), 1994; 169.

3 Ibid., 165.

4 The parables of Jesus often challenge the reader to change his or her approach to God and fellow human beings. For further reading on this topic, see Arthur E. Zannoni, *Jesus of the Gospels: Teacher, Storyteller, Friend, Messiah* (Cincinnati: St. Anthony Messenger Press, 1996), 65–84.

5 John R. Donahue, *The Gospel in Parable* (Minneapolis: Fortress Press, 1988), 83.

6 Ibid., 149.

7 Ibid., 155.

8 Robert H. Stein. *An Introduction to the Parables of Jesus* (Philadelphia: Westminster Press, 1981), 123.

9 Rudolph Otto, *The Idea of the Holy* (London: Oxford University Press), 1950.

10 For further reading on this topic, see Zannoni, *Jesus of the Gospels*, 55–63.

# Chapter five

1 Elizabeth A. Johnson, *She Who Is* (New York: Crossroad, 1994), 82–83. Also see George Montague, *The Holy Spirit: Growth of a Biblical Tradition* (New York: Paulist, 1976).

2 On the role of the "spirit" in the Genesis creation stories, see Conrad Hyers, *The Meaning of Creation: Genesis and Modern Science* (Atlanta: John Knox Press, 1984).

3 For a thorough treatment of the role of the spirit in the prophet Balaam, see Arthur E. Zannoni, "Balaam: International Seer/Wizard Prophet," *St. Luke's Journal of Theology* 22 (December 1978): 5–19.

4 Raymond E. Brown offers a detailed analysis of the Paraclete in an appendix of his commentary on the Gospel, volume 2. See Raymond E. Brown, *The Gospel According to John* (New York: Doubleday, 1966, 1970). In addition, Brown treats the topic of the Paraclete in his *An Introduction to the New Testament* (New York: Doubleday, 1997), 351–356.

5 For an encyclopedic presentation of the role of the Holy Spirit in the Gospel of Luke see G. W. H. Lampe "The Holy Spirit in the Writings of St. Luke" in *Studies in the Gospels* (Oxford: Oxford University Press, 1967), 159–200.

# Bibliography

*Anchor Bible Dictionary* (Volume 2), New York: Doubleday, 1992. s.v. "God."

Armstrong, Karen. *A History of God.* New York: Balentine Books, 1994.

Balentine, Samuel E. *The Hidden God.* Oxford: Oxford University Press, 1983.

Buber, Martin. *The Prophetic Faith.* New York: Macmillan, 1949.

————. *Moses—The Revelation and the Covenant.* New York: Harper & Row, 1958.

Donohue, John R. *The Gospel in Parable.* Minneapolis: Fortress Press, 1998.

*Harper's Bible Dictionary*, Paul J. Achtemeier (ed.) San Francisco: Harper & Row Publishers, 1985. s.v. "Names of God in the Old Testament," "Names of God in the New Testament," and "God."

Johnson, Elizabeth A. *She Who Is: The Mystery of God in Feminist Theological Discourse.* New York: Crossroad, 1992.

Longman, Tremper, and Reid, Daniel G. *God Is a Warrior.* Carlisle: Paternoster, 1995.

McKenzie, John L. *Dictionary of the Bible.* Milwaukee: Bruce Publishing Co., 1965. s.v. "God."

Mays, James L. *The Lord Reigns.* Louisville: Westminster John Knox, 1994.

Miles, J. *God: A Biography.* New York: Simon & Schuster, 1995.

Mills, Mary E. *Images of God in the Old Testament.* Collegeville, Minnesota: Liturgical Press, 1998.

Montague, George. *The Holy Spirit: Growth of a Biblical Tradition.* New York: Paulist, 1976.

Murphy, Roland E. *The Tree of Life: An Exposition of Biblical Wisdom Literature.* New York: Doubleday, 1990.

Murray, John Courtney. *The Problem of God.* New Haven, Connecticut: Yale University Press, 1964.

Niehaus, Jeffrey J. *God at Sinai.* Carlisle: Paternoster, 1995.

Otto, Rudolph. *The Idea of the Holy.* London: Oxford University Press, 1950.

Sasso, Sandy Eisenberg. *In God's Name.* Woodstock, Vermont: Jewish Lights Publishing, 1994.

Smith, Mark S. *The Early History of God.* New York: Harper & Row, 1990.

Shermis, Michael, and Zannoni, Arthur E. (eds.). *Introduction to Jewish-Christian Relations.* New York: Paulist Press, 1991.

Stein, Robert H. *An Introduction to the Parables of Jesus.* Philadelphia: Westminster, 1981.

Thomas, Carolyn. *Will the Real God Please Stand Up?* New York: Paulist Press, 1991.

Trible, Phyllis. *God and the Rhetoric of Sexuality.* Philadelphia: Fortress, 1978.

Vardy, Peter. *The Puzzle of God.* London: HarperCollins, 1990.

Westermann, Claus. *What Does the Old Testament Say About God?* Atlanta: John Knox, 1979.

Winter, Miriam Therese. *Woman Praying, Woman Song—Resources for Ritual.* New York: Meyer Stone, 1987.

———— *Woman Wisdom—A Feminist Lectionary and Psalter. Part 1: Women in the Hebrew Scripture.* New York: Crossroad, 1993.

Wren, Brian. *What Language Shall I Borrow? God Talk in Worship: A Male Response to Feminist Theology.* New York: Crossroad, 1991.

Zannoni, Arthur E. *Jesus of the Gospels: Teacher, Storyteller, Friend, Messiah.* Cincinnati, Ohio: St. Anthony Messenger Press, 1996.

———— *The Old Testament: A Bibliography.* Collegeville, Minnesota: Liturgical Press, 1992.

# Index of Scripture